© **Scrapbooking Coach 2022**

All Rights Reserved

No part of this book or any of its contents may be reproduced, copied, modified or adapted, without prior written consent of the author, unless otherwise indicated for standalone materials.

Legal Notice

The author retains the right to change this guide at any time. This guide is for information purposes only and the author doesn't accept any responsibilities for any liabilities resulting from the use of this information. The reader assumes all responsibility for the use of the information herein.

CLAIM YOUR FREE BONUS GIFT!

As our way of saying thank you for your purchase, we want to give you a **very special gift** to help you in your scrapbooking.

To get your FREE gift from us, just visit this special page on our website:

www.scrapbookingcoach.com/gift

Table of Contents

A Note from Anna	4
How To Get The Most Out Of This Book	5
One Photo Sketches	6
Two Photo Sketches	35
Three Photo Sketches	55
Four Photo Sketches	73
Double-Page Sketches	91

Welcome to *525 New And Advanced Scrapbooking Sketches - Volume 2!*

In 2014, we released volume 1 of 525 New And Inspiring Scrapbooking Sketches. We didn't realize it at the time, but this book would go on to become a *bestseller* in the world of scrapbooking!

After a lot of positive feedback from scrappers all over the world, releasing a follow-up book was a total no brainer.

So here it is: **525 New And Advanced Scrapbooking Sketches Volume 2.**

525 totally new and unique sketches that are different from the ones in the first book!

Each sketch in this book is guaranteed to help you create a gorgeous looking page that you'll be proud of!

As I said in the introduction of the first volume: I wish you nothing but *fun and excitement* with your scrapbooking!

Also, if you have any feedback or perhaps a testimonial about how 525 New And Advanced Scrapbooking Sketches - Volume 2 has helped you, I would love to hear from you.

Please reach out and send me an email at: helpdesk@scrapbookingcoach.com

Thank you for putting your trust in us and purchasing this book. I hope that you'll love the layout ideas in this book as much as we do.

Be inspired to creatively preserve your most precious memories, now and always!

Anna Lyons

How To Get The Most Out Of This Book

Each chapter inside the 525 New And Advanced Scrapbooking Sketches - Volume 2, showcases sketches by the number of photos you can arrange.

For example, if you have three photos to work with, browse the chapter that has sketches with three photos until you find a sketch that you like.

Once you've decided on a sketch, prepare your craft stash so you have all the necessary page elements to start scrapbooking!

You can follow each element according to the sketch, build the layers up, and watch your page come to life! *But don't limit yourself!* You can tweak and adjust each sketch as you please and create a scrapbook page masterpiece.

Use this sketch...

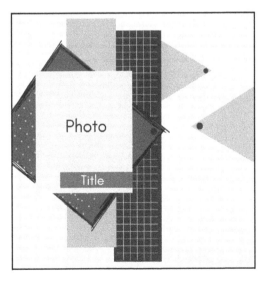

...to create this gorgeous page!

One Photo Sketches

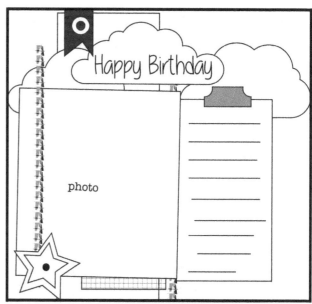

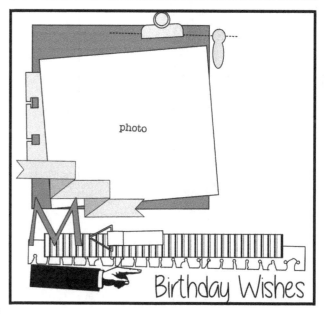

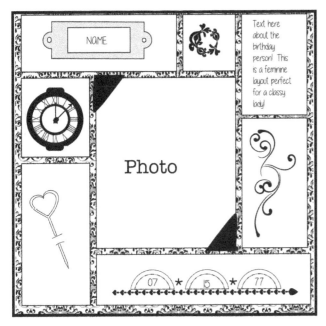

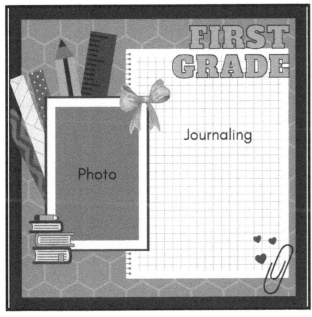
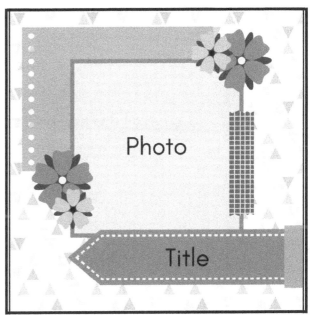

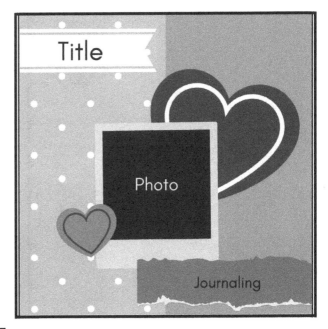

7

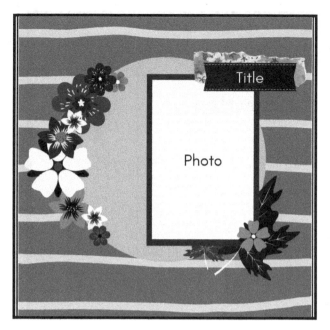

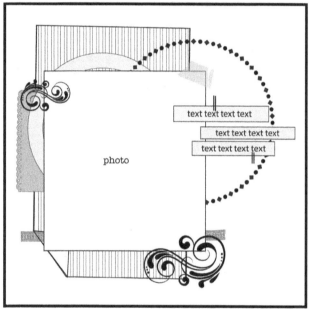

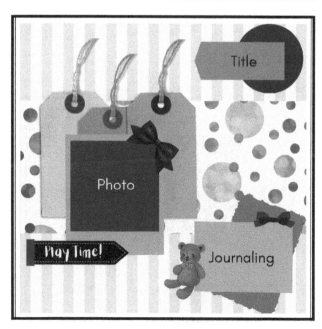
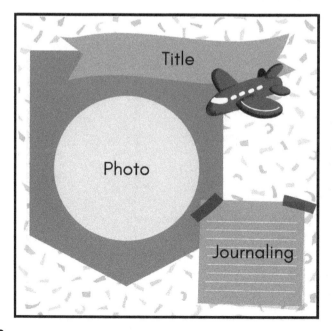

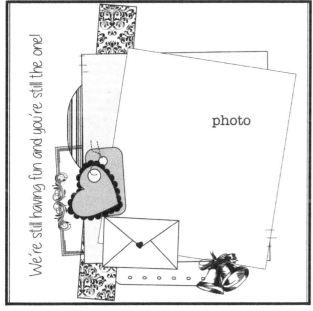

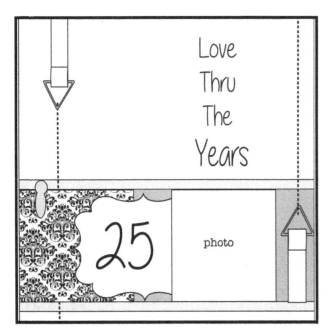

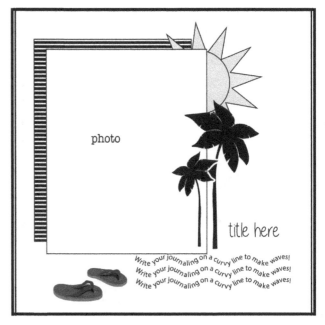

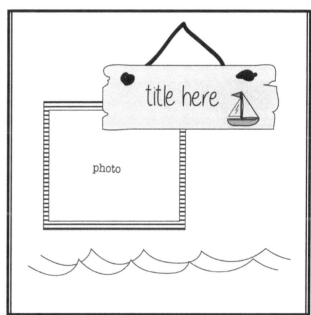

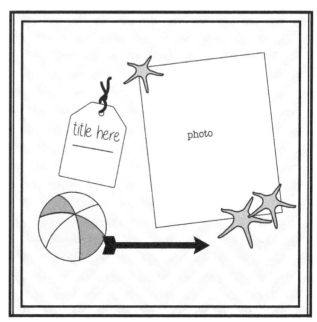

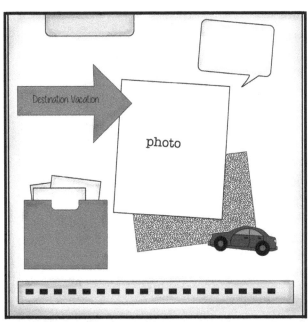
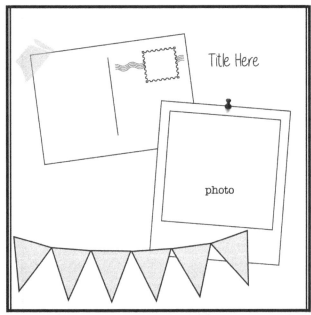
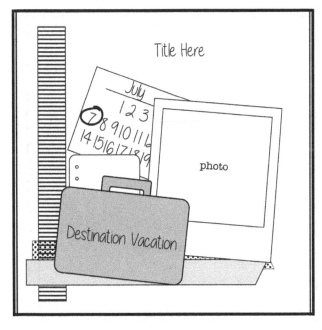
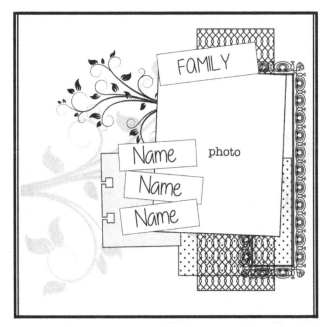

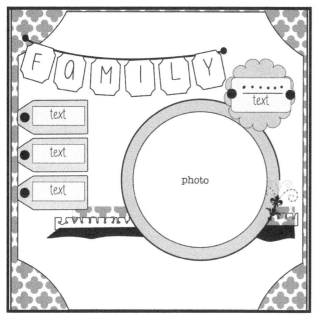

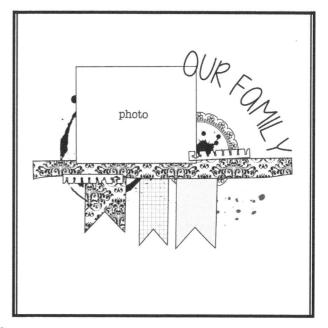

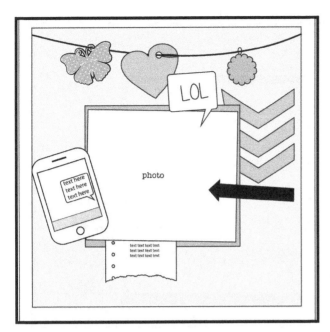
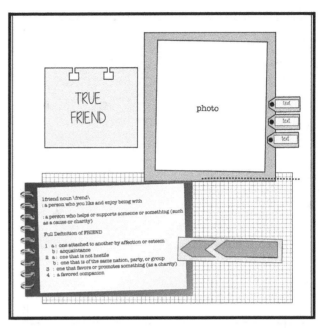

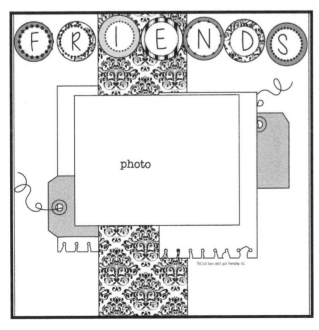
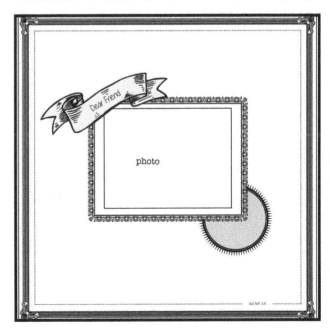

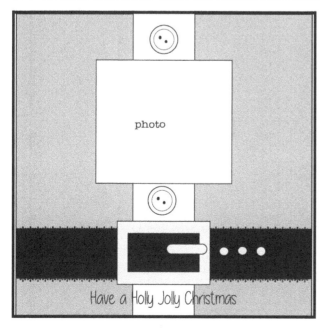

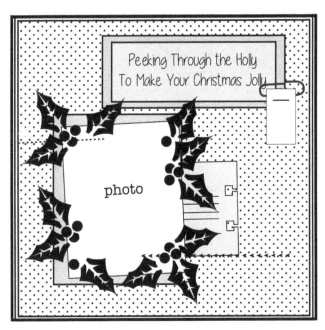

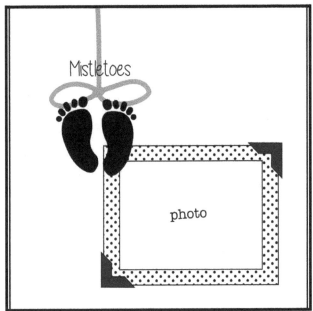

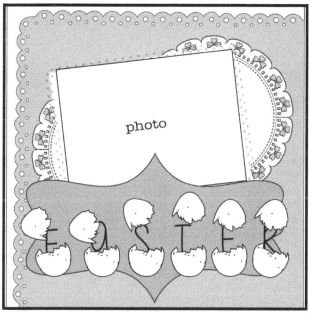
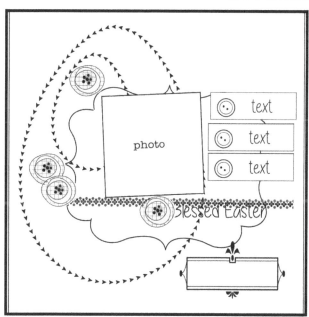
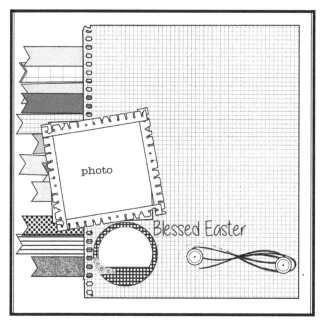
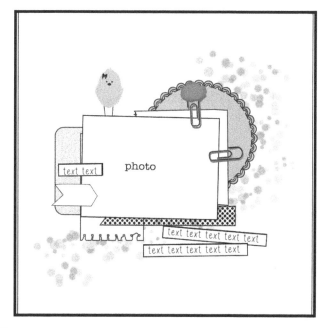

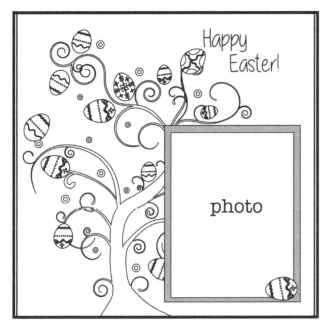

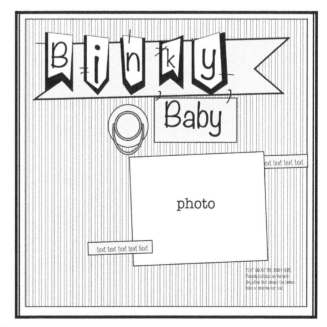

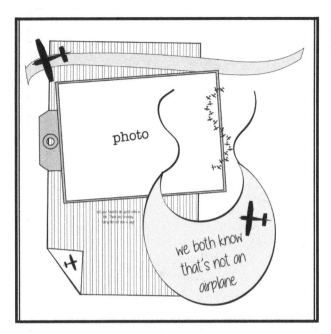

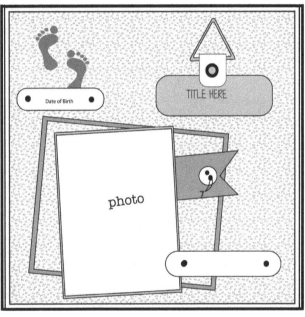

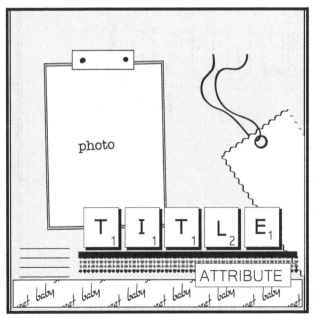

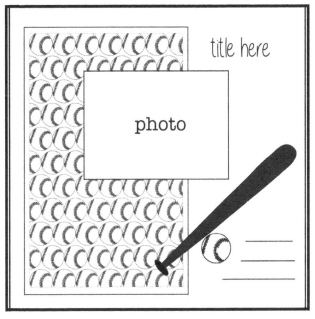
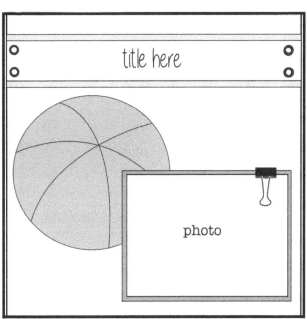
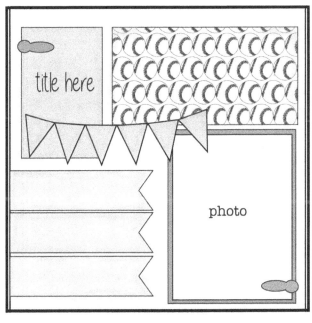

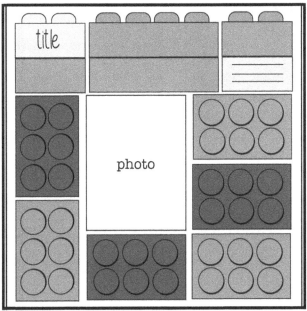
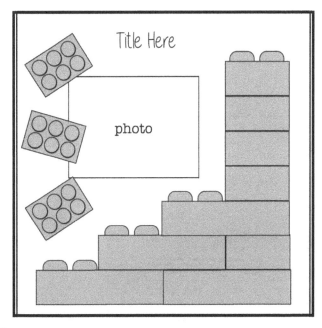

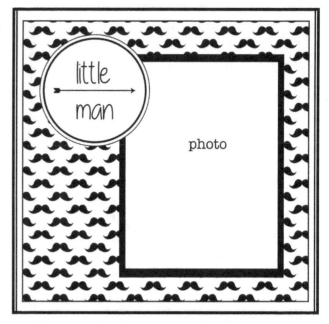

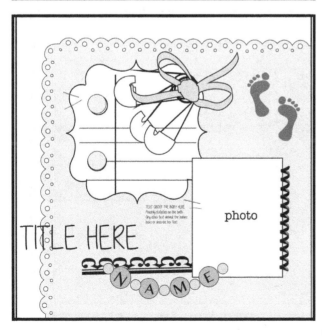
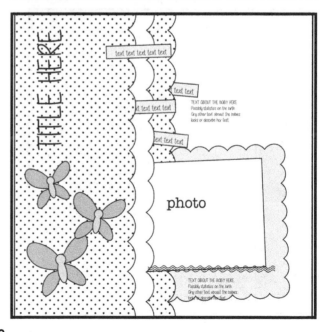

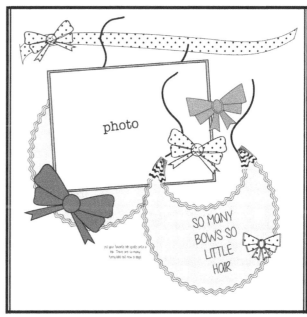
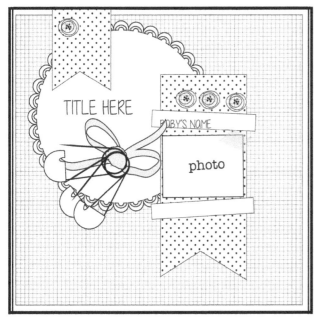
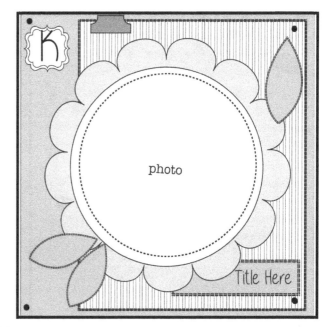

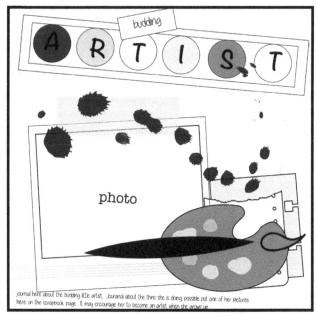
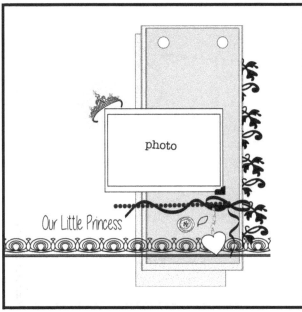

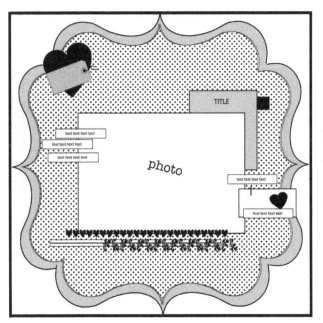
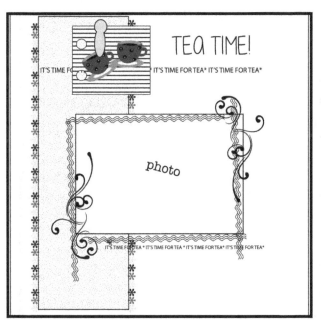

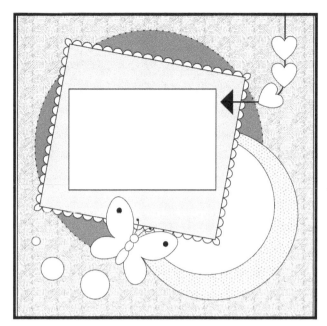

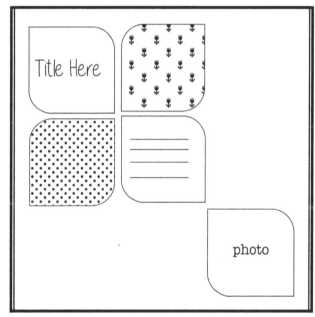
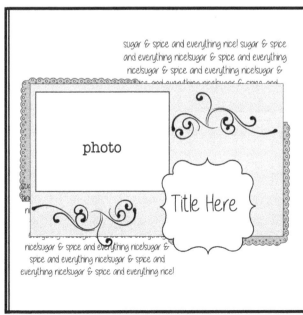
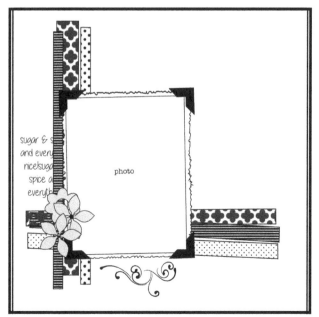

25

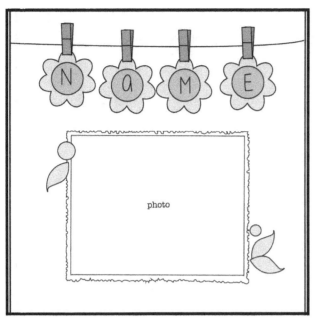

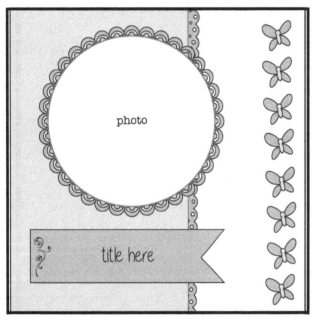

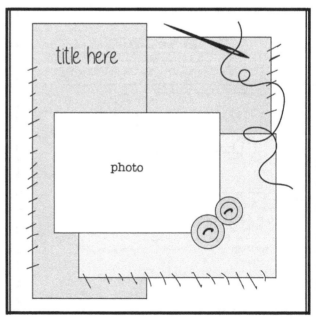

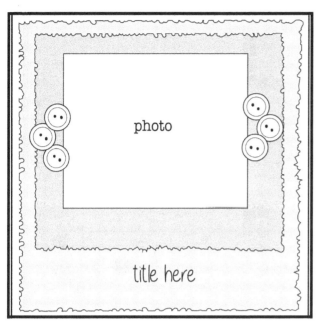

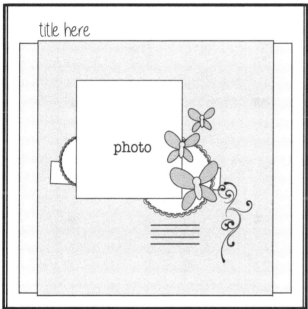
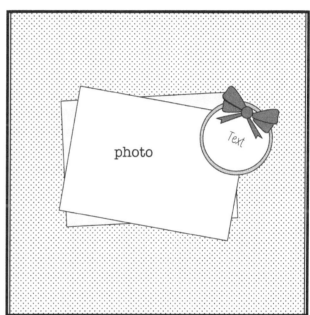

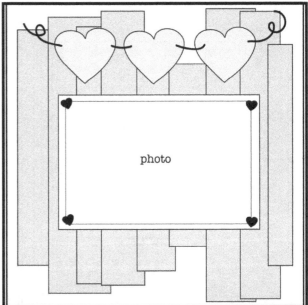

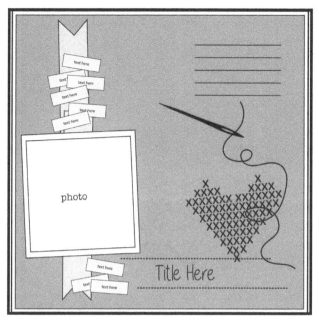
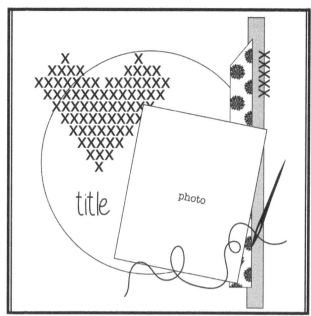

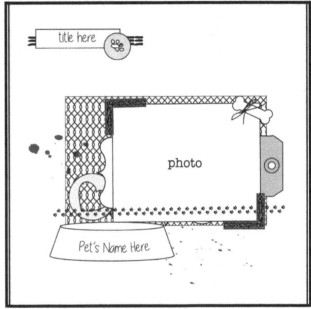

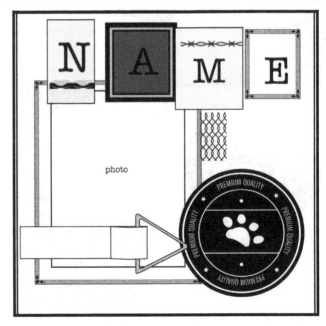

30

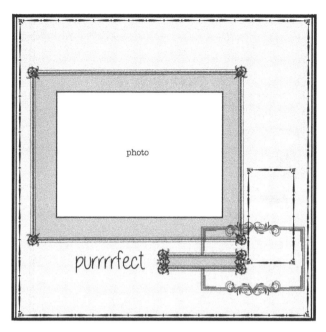
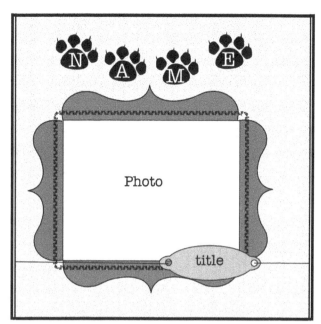
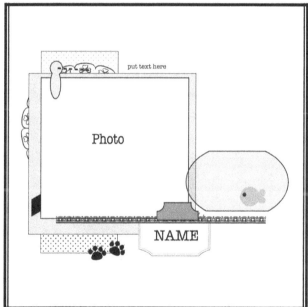

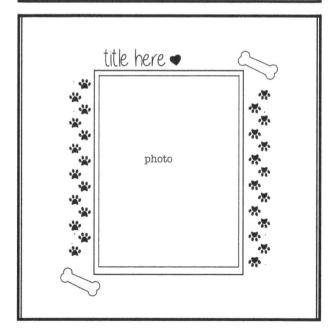
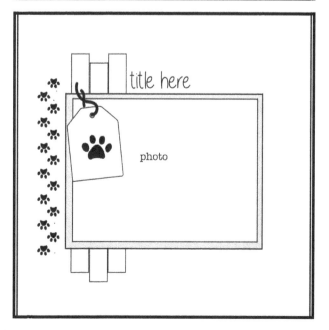

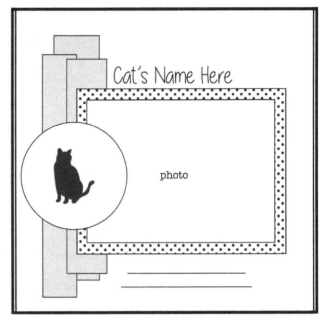
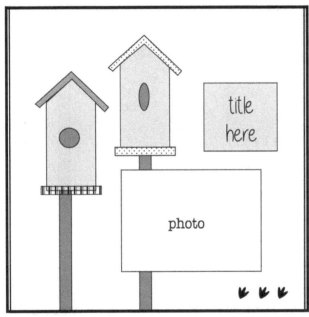

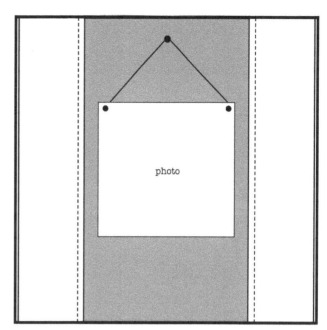

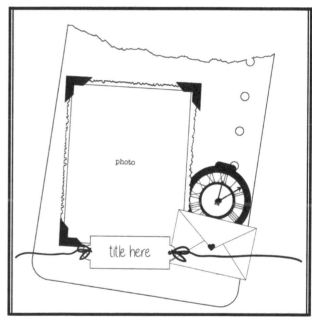

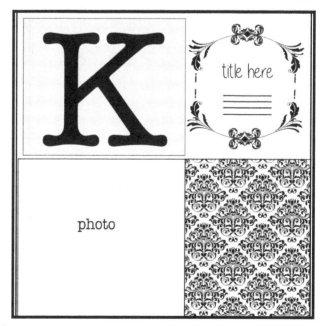

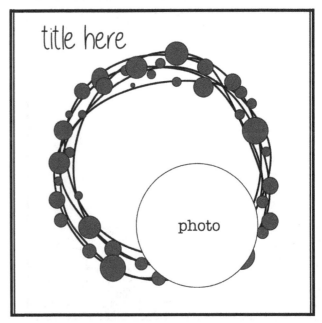

Two Photo Sketches

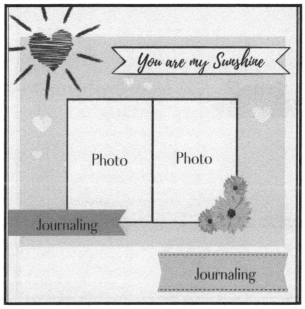

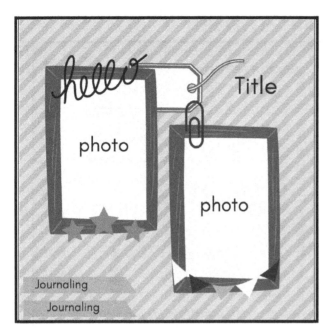
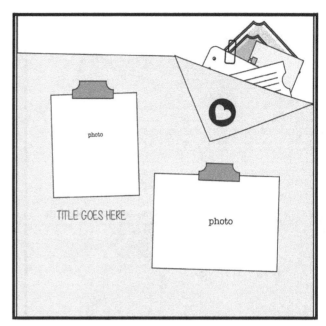

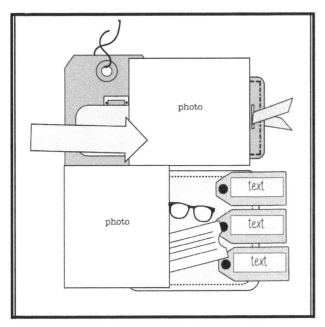
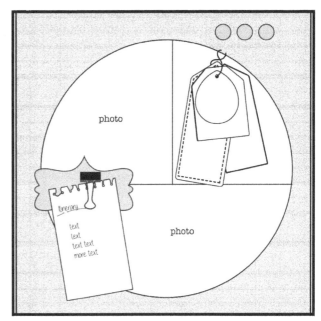

37

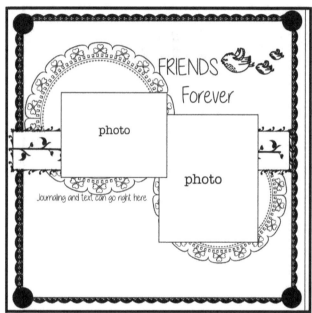
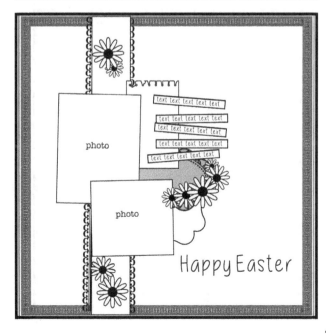
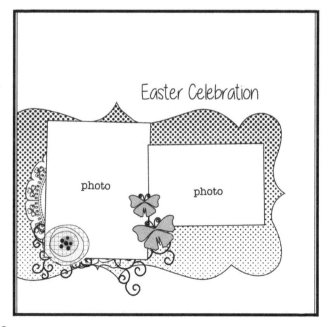

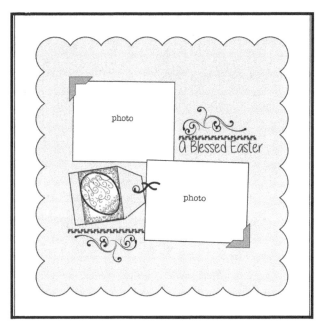
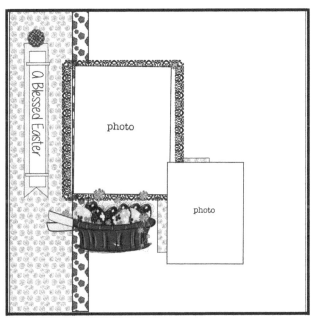
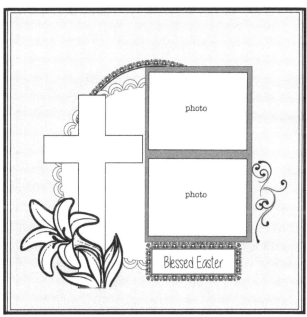
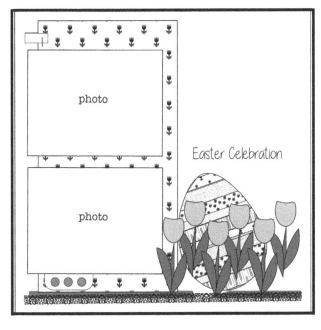

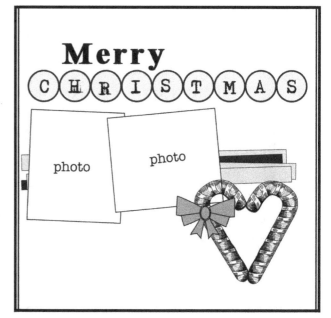

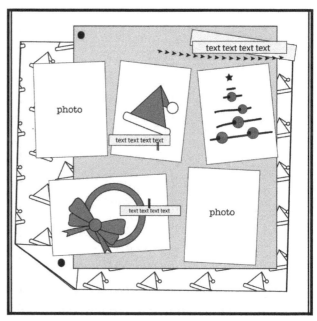

40

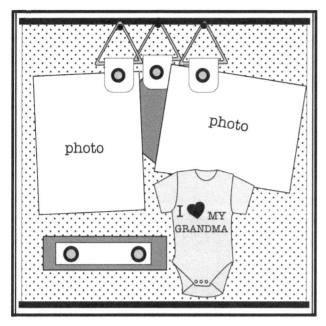
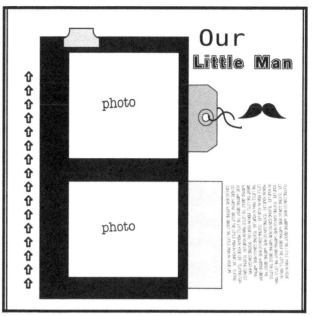
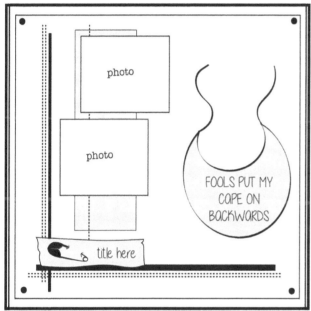
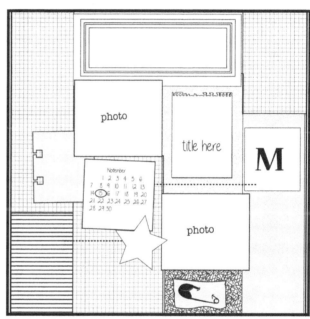

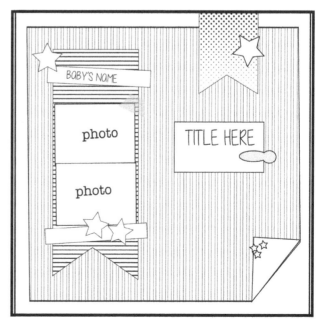

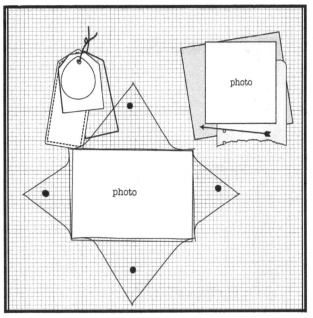
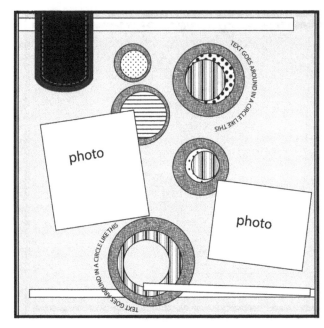
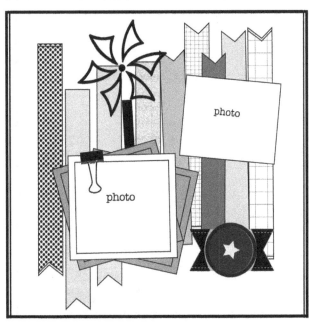
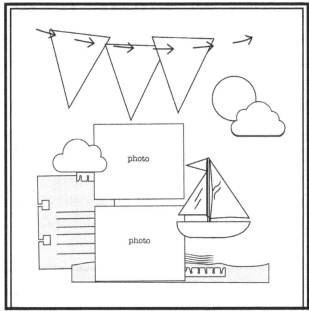
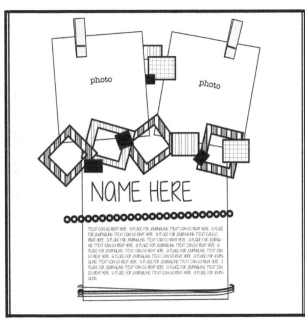

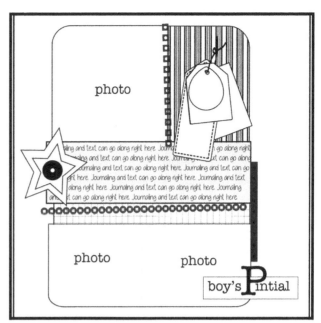
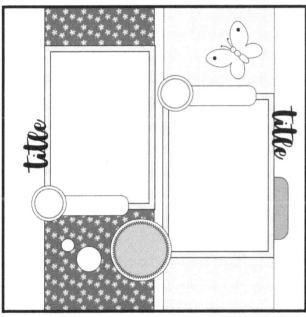
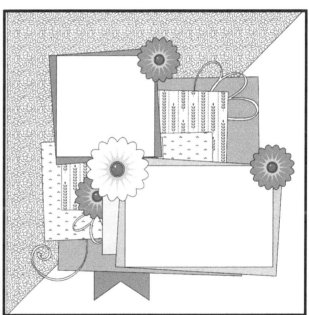

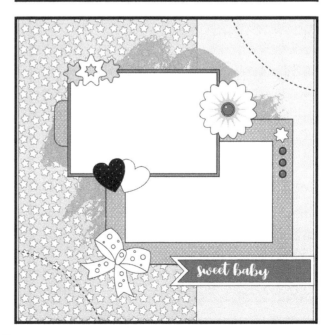

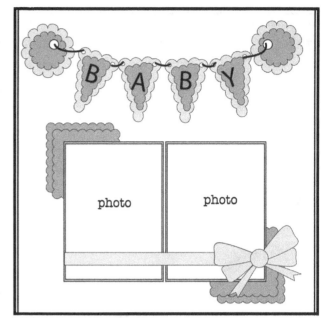
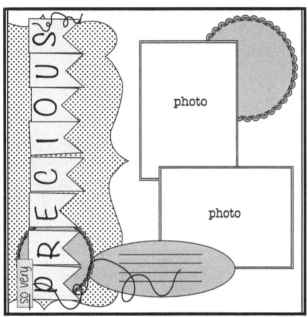
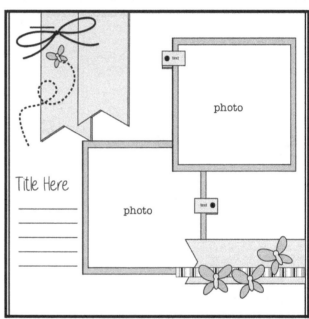
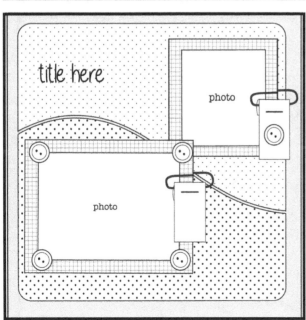
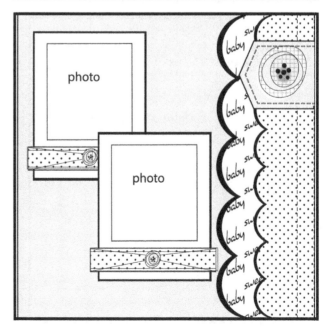

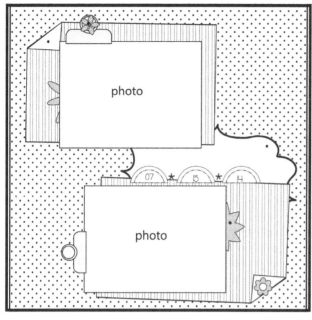
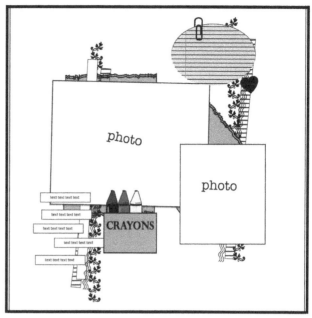

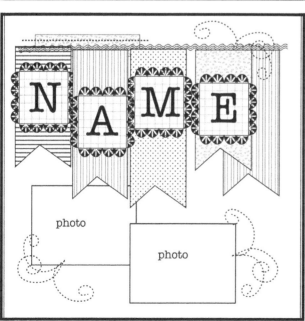
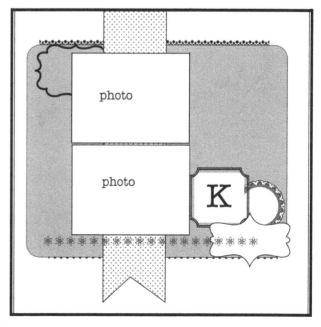

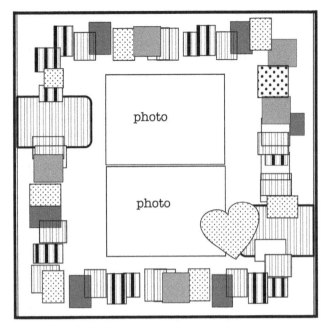
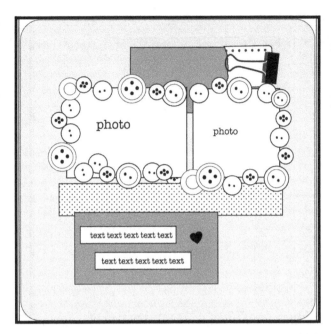

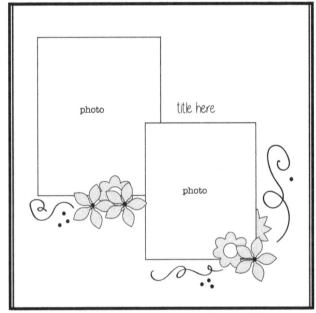

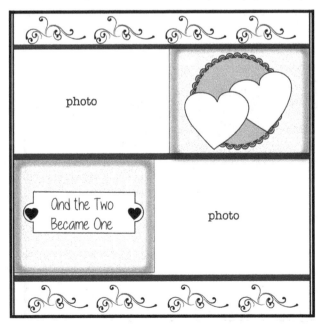

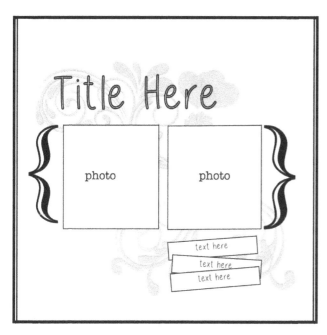
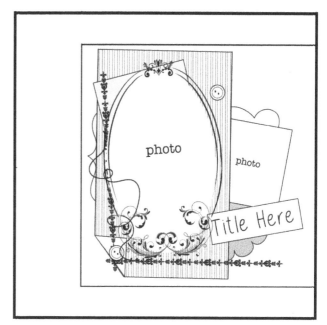

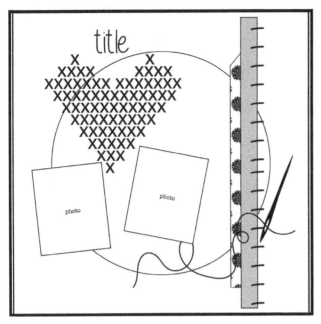

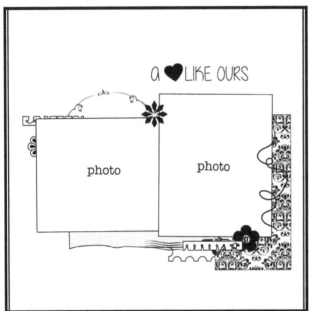
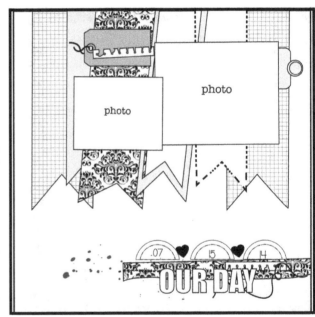

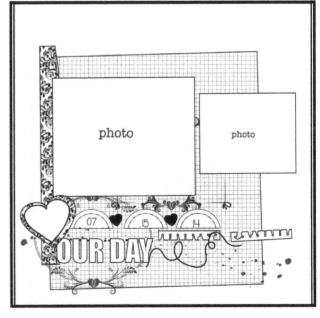

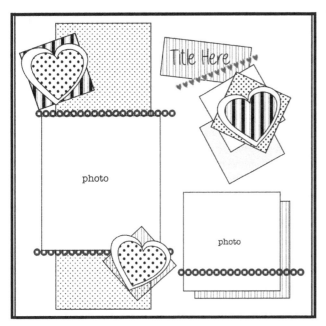
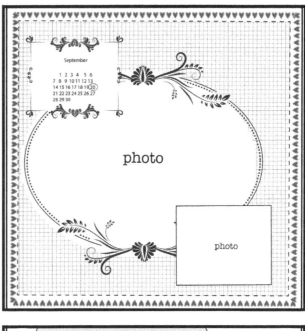
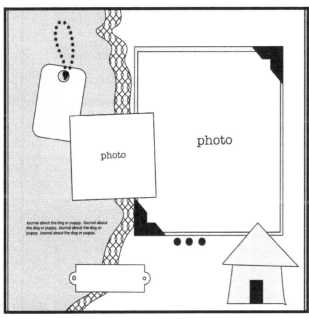
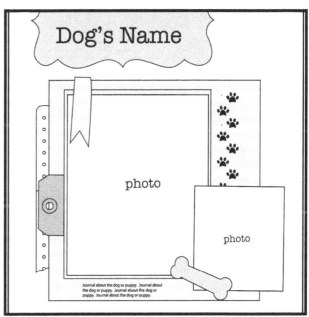

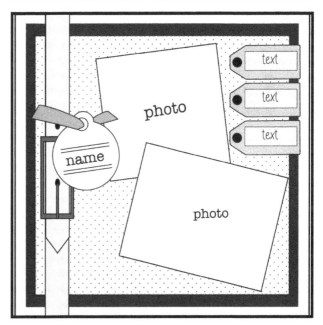

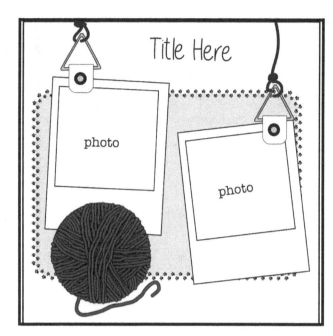

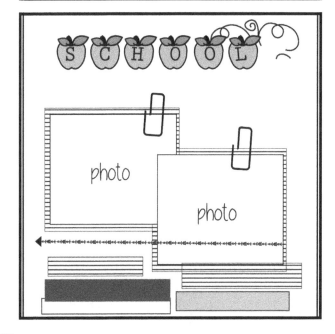

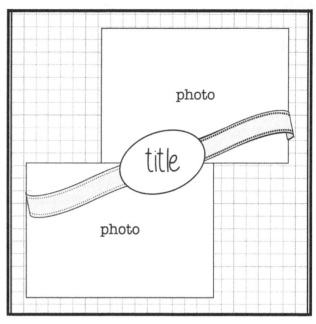
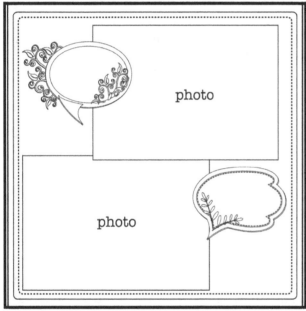
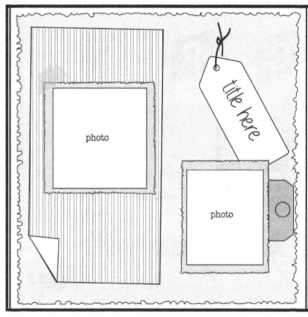
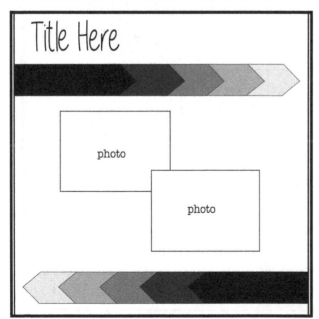
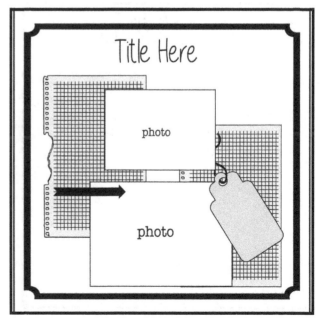

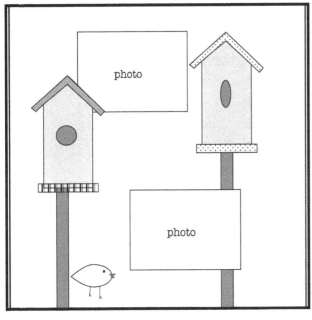
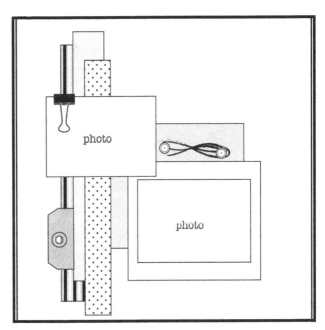

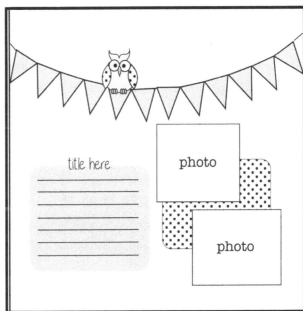
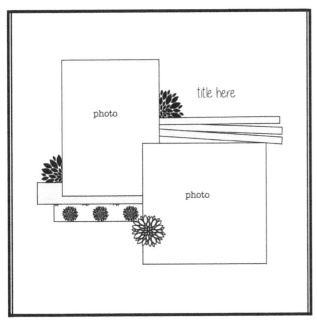

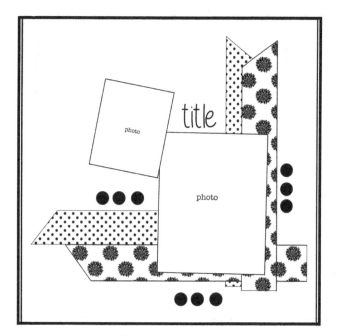
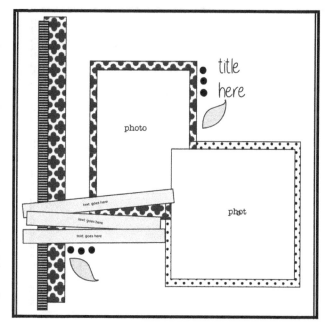

Three Photo Sketches

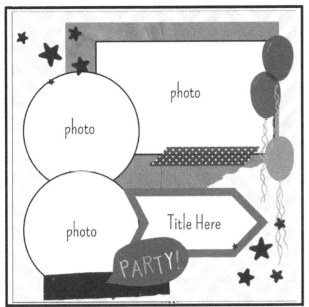

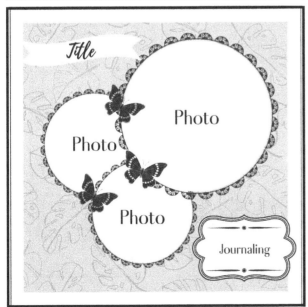
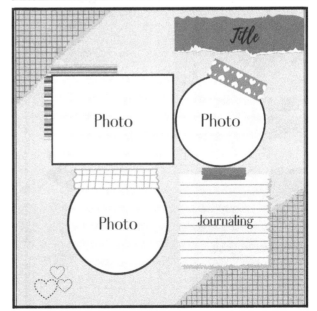

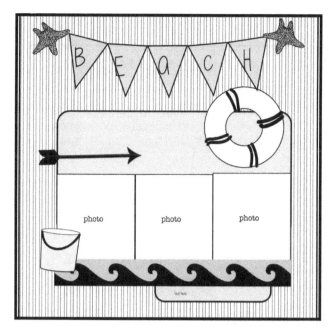

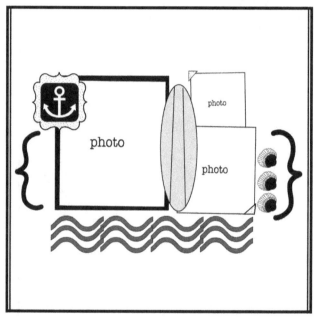

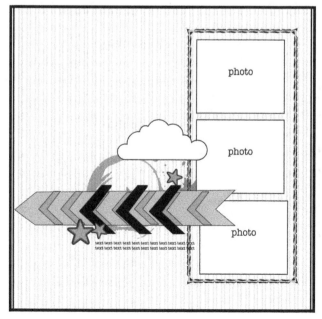

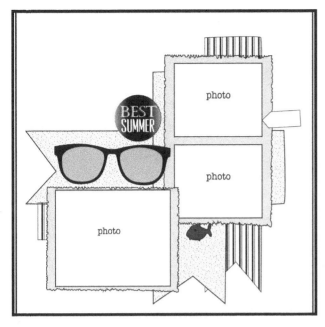
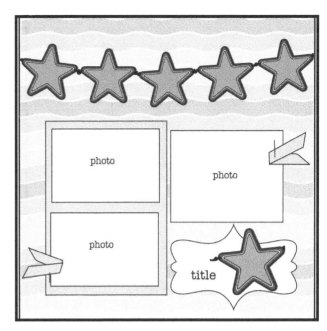

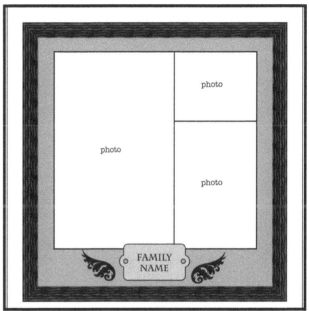

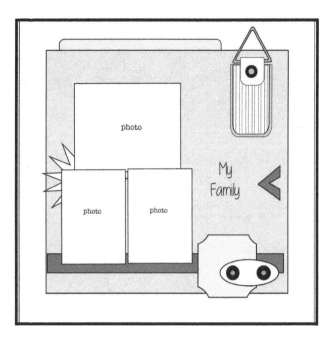
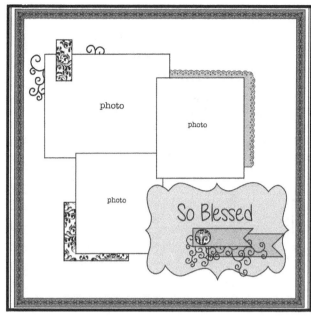

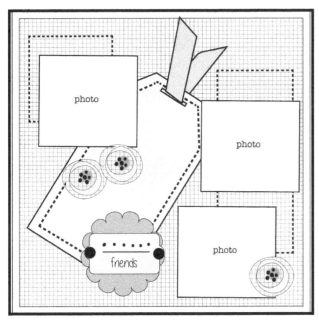
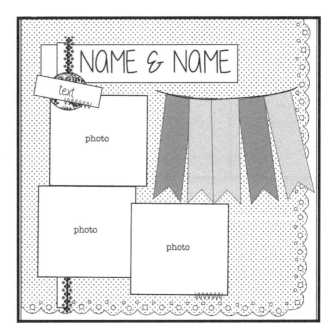
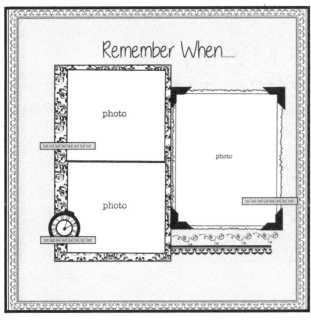
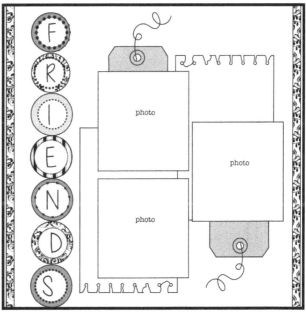

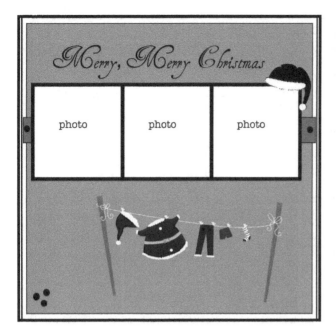
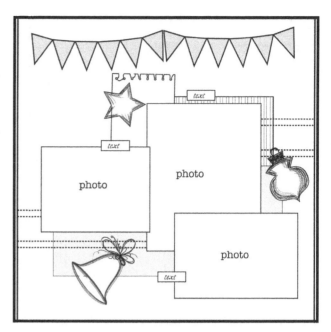

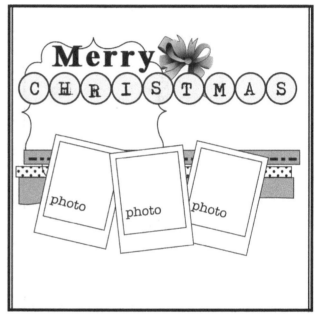

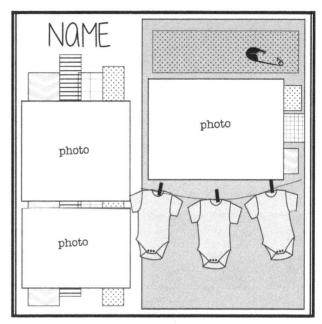
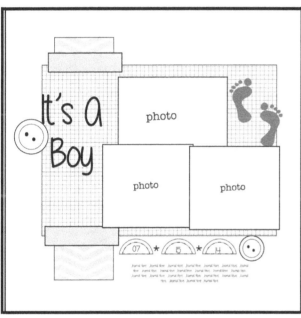
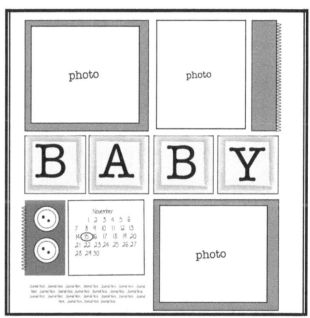
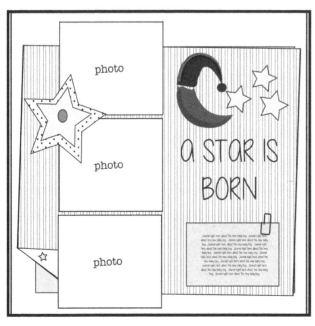

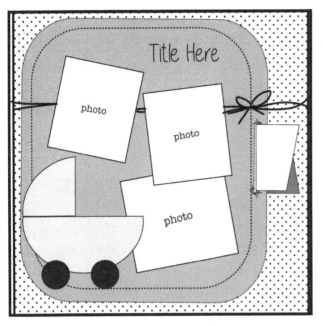

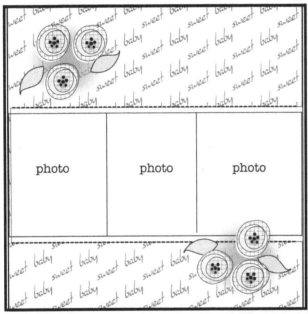

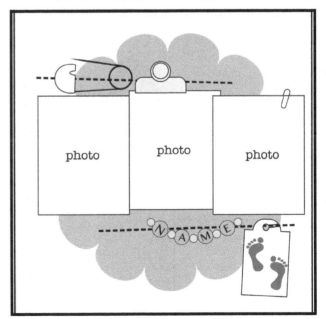

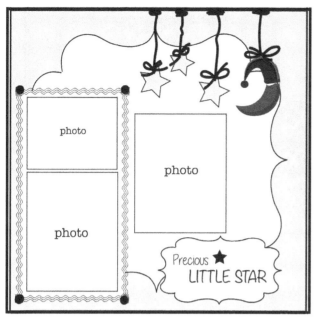
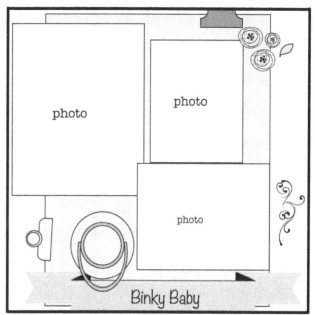
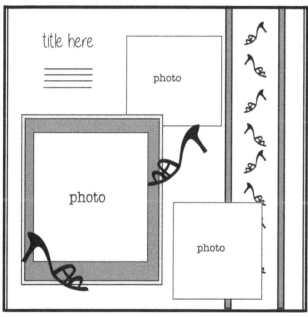

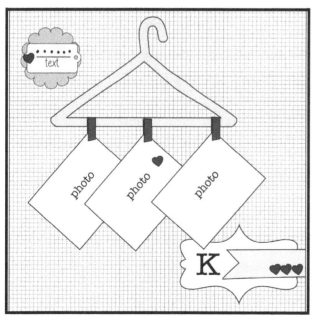
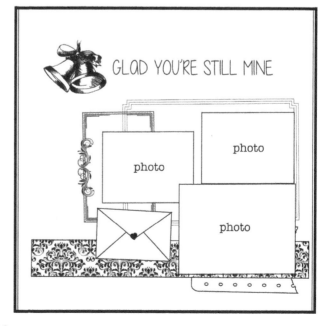

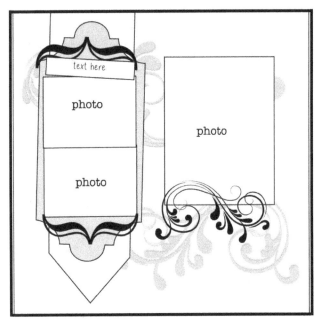
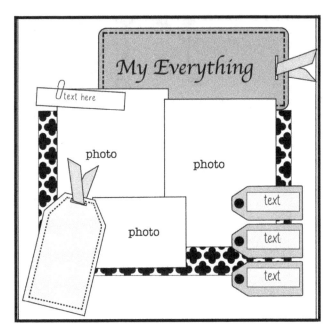
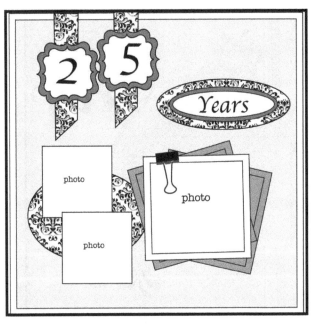
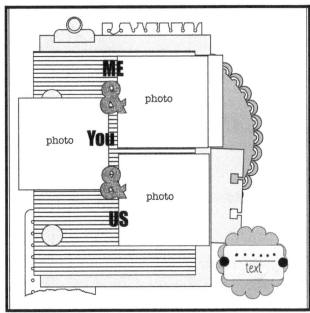
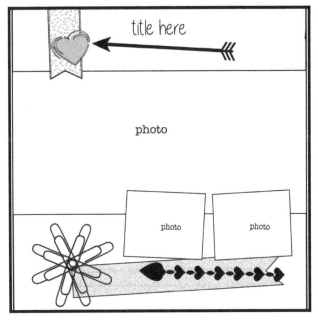

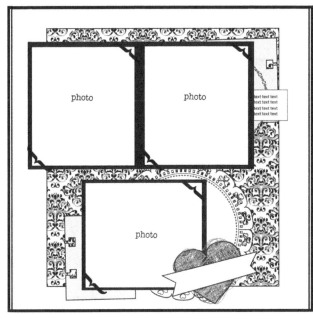
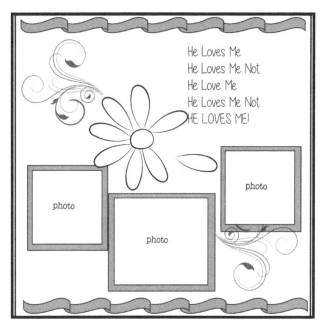

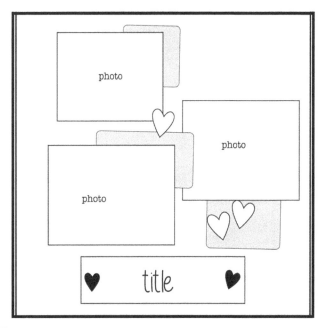

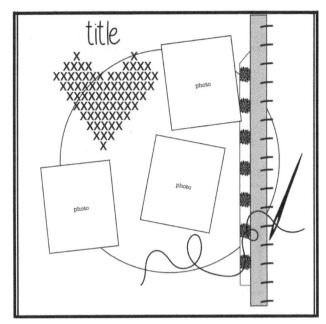

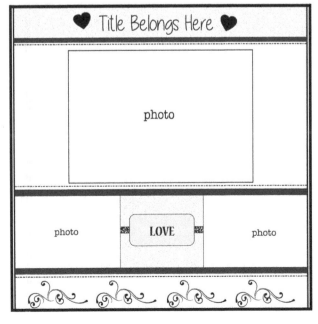
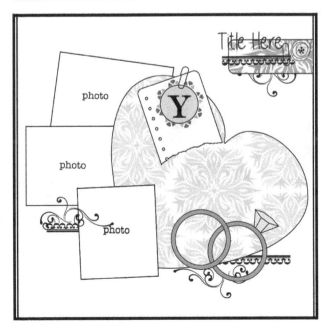

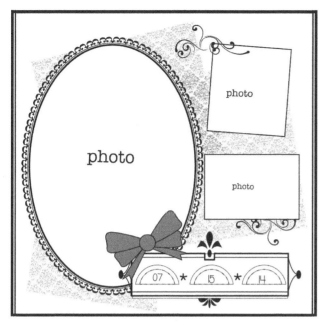

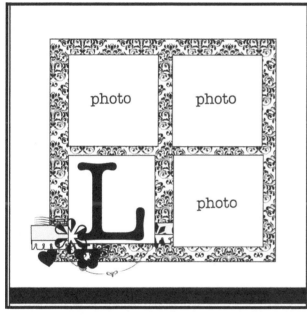
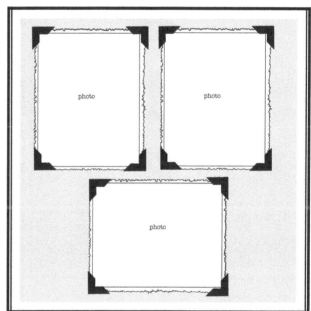
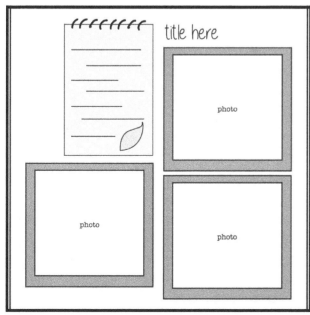

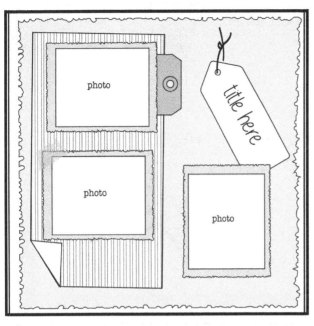

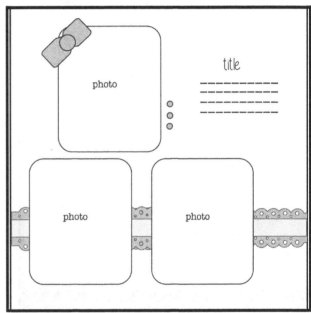
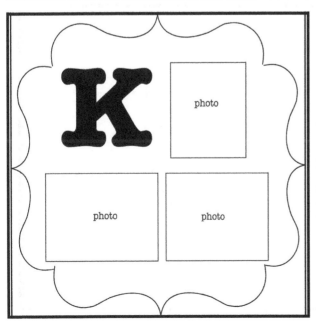
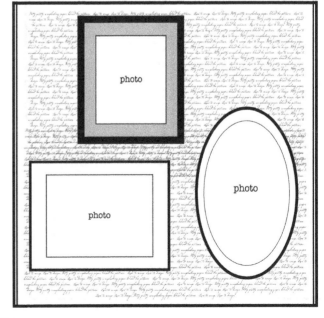

68

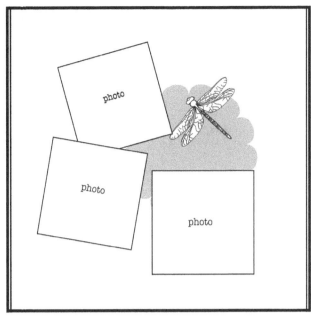
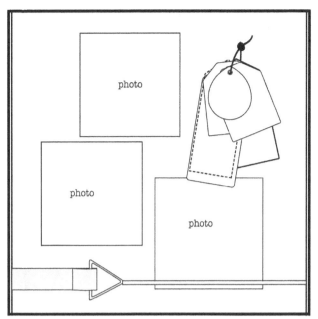
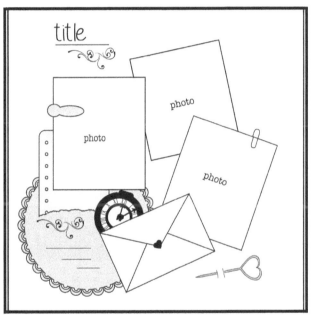
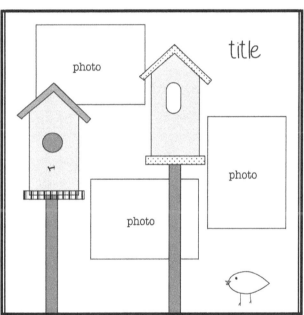
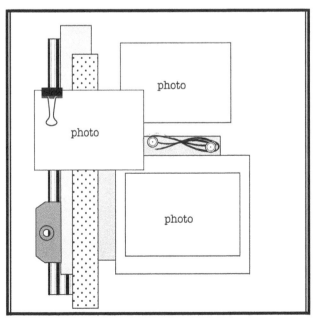

69

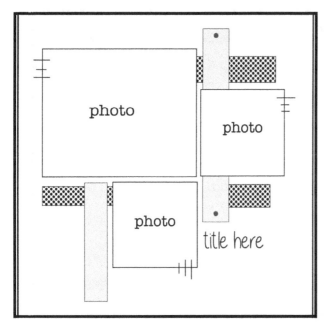

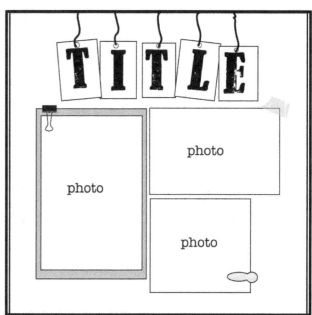

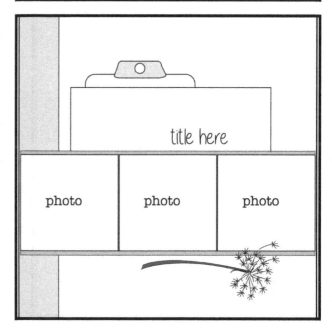

70

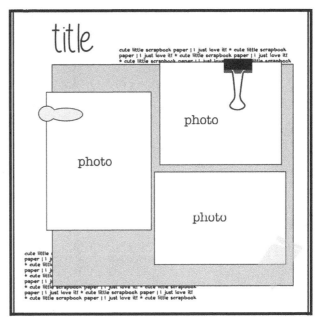
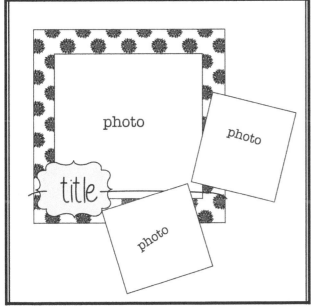

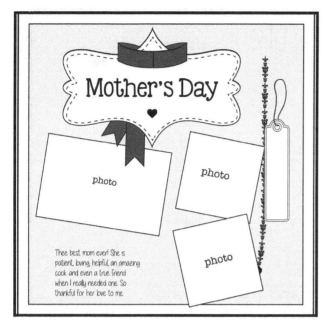
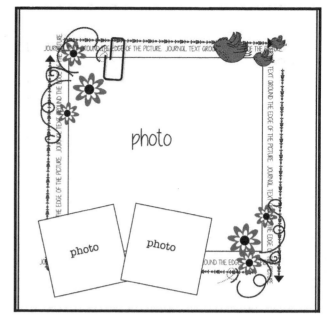

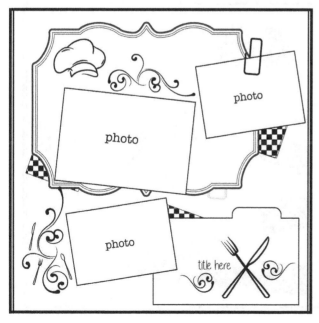
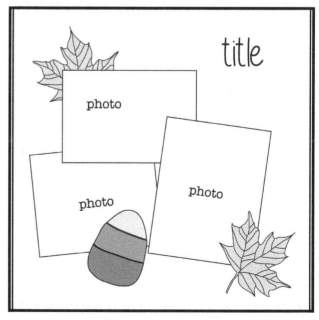

Four Photo Sketches

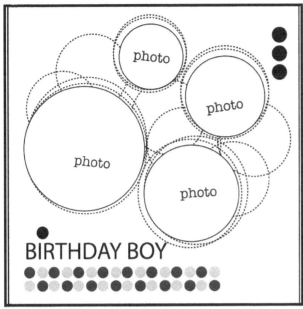

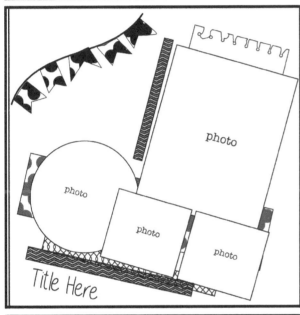
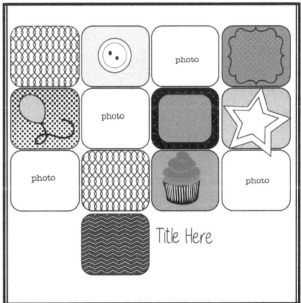
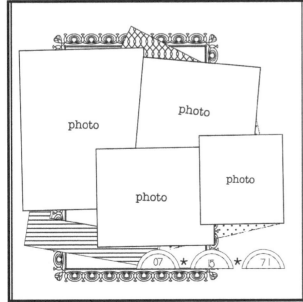
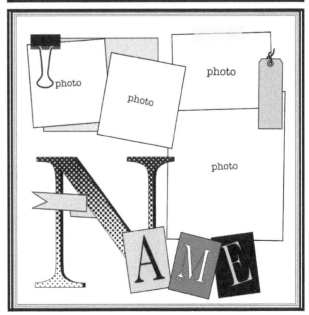

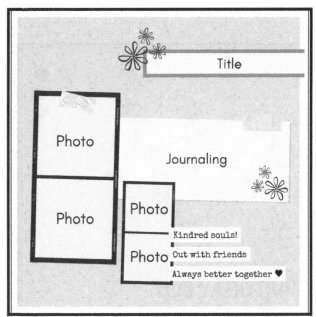

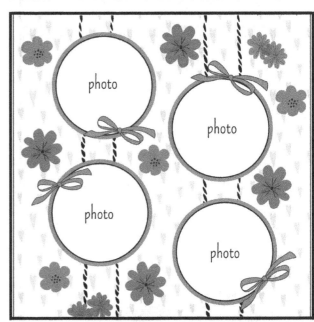
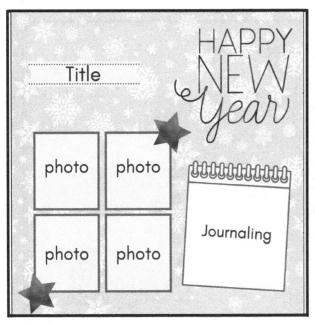
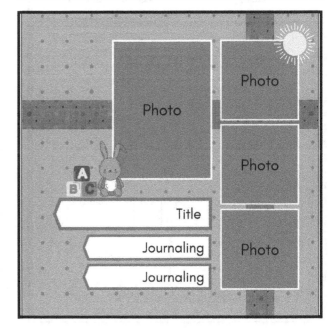

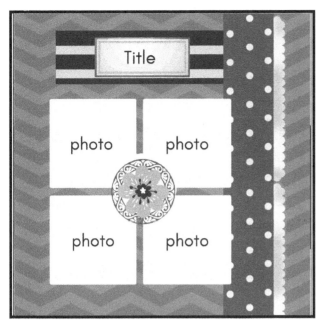

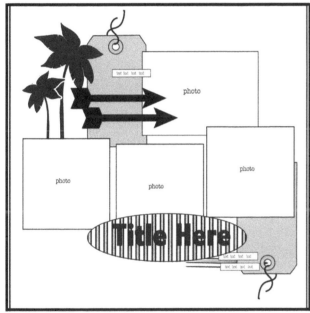
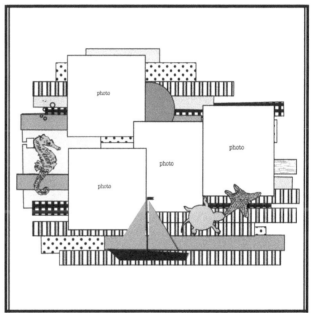

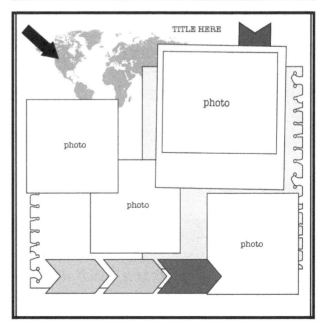

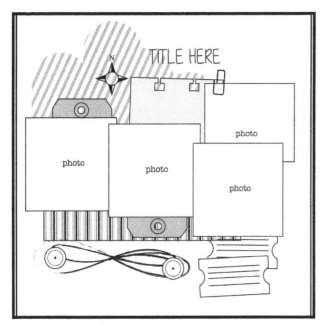

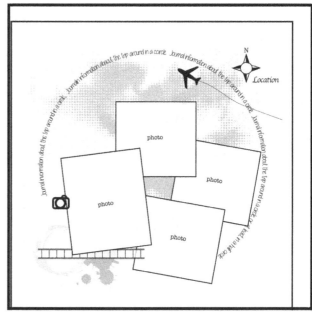

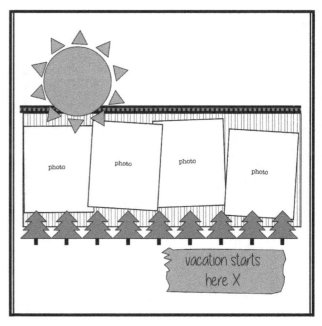

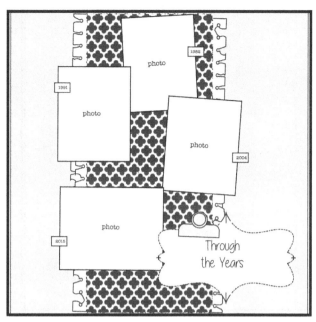

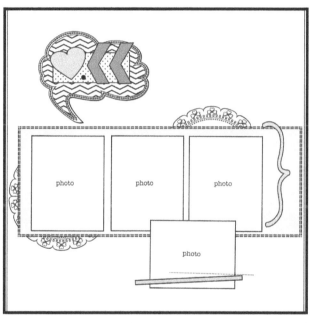

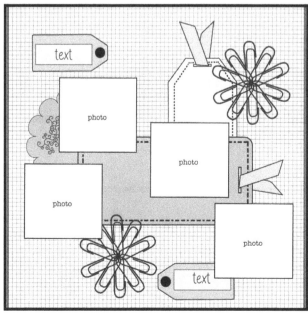
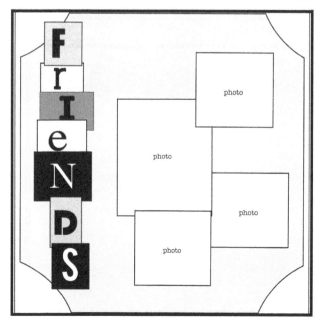

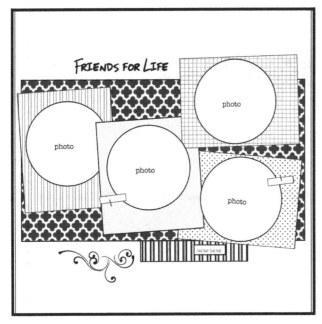
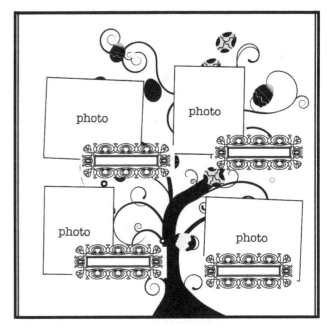
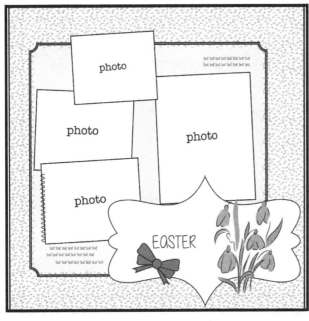
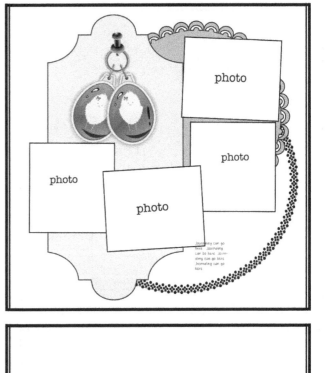
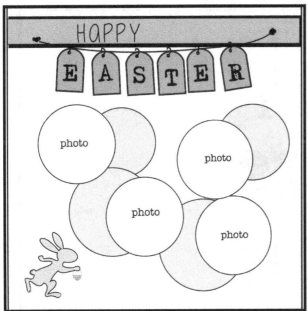
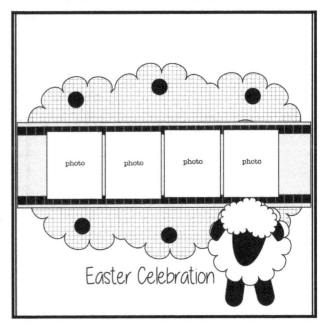

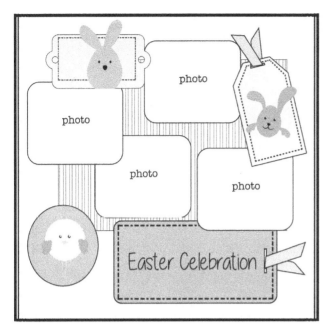
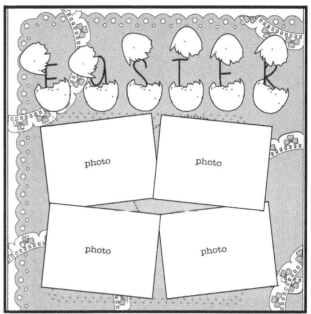

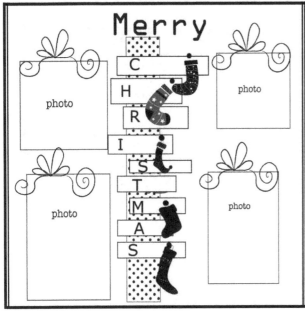
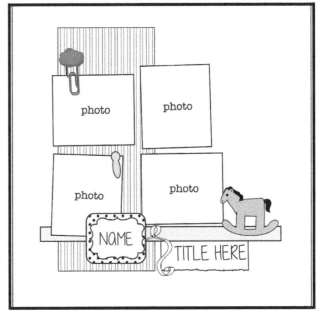
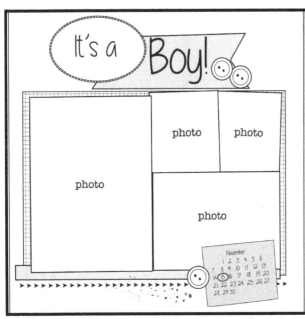

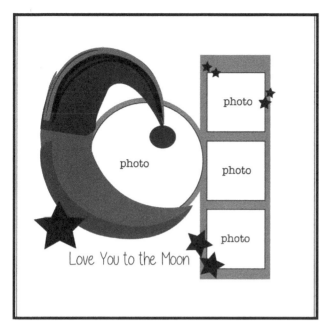
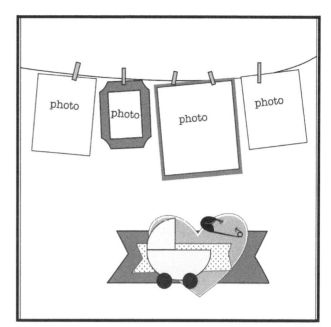
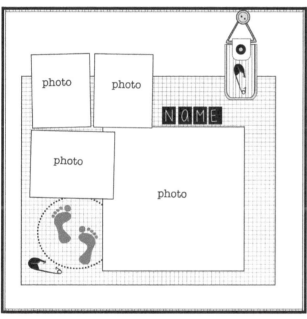
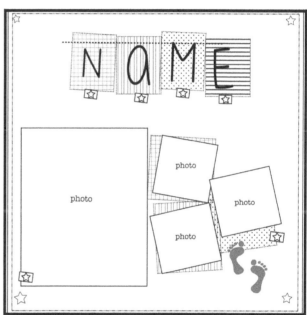
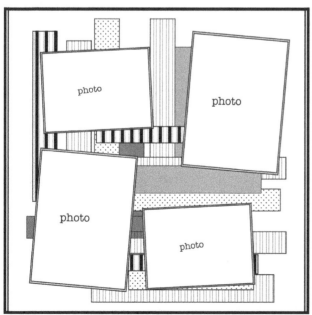
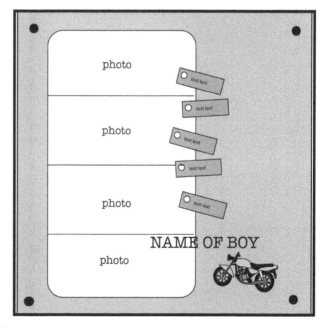

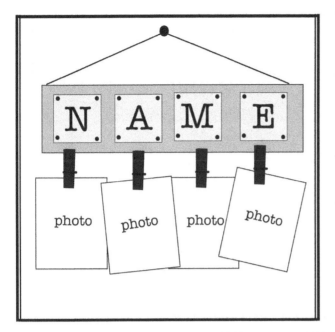
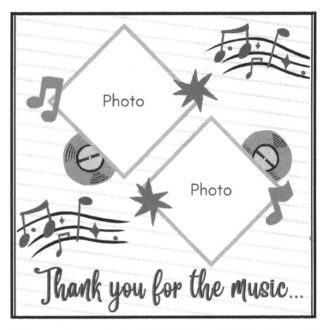
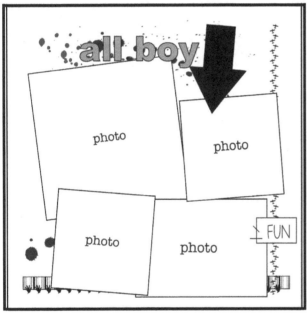
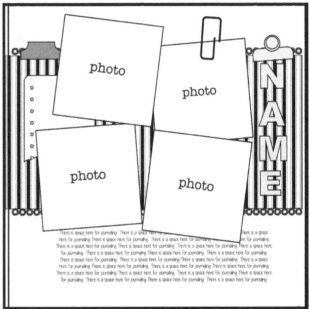
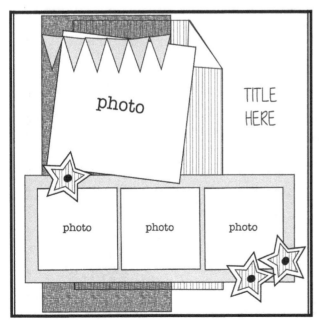
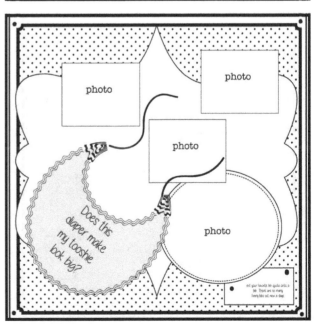

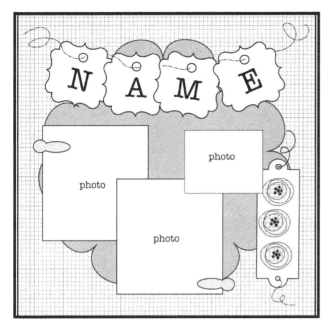
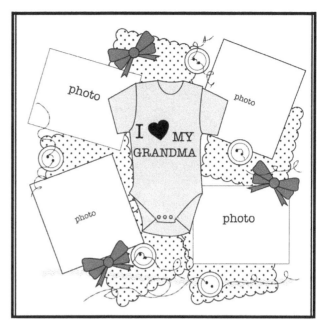
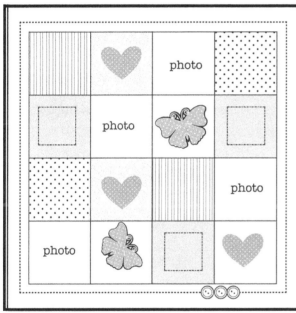

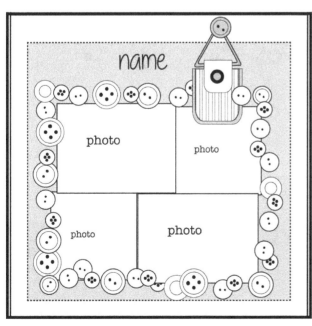
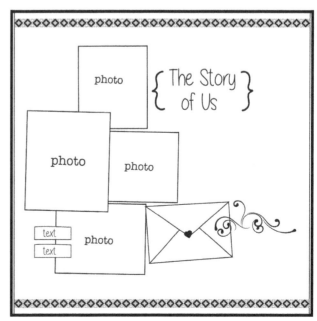

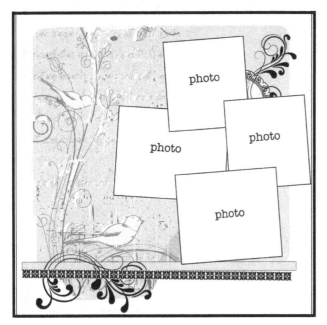

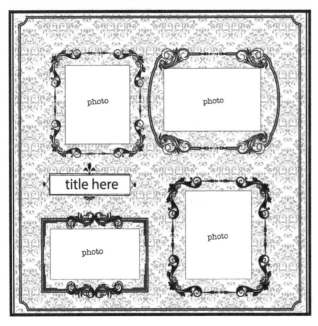

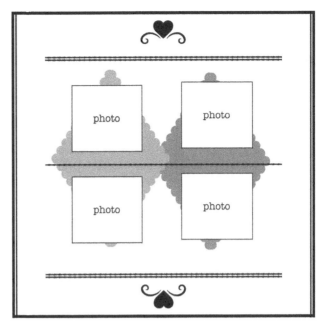
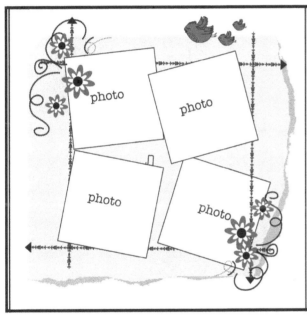

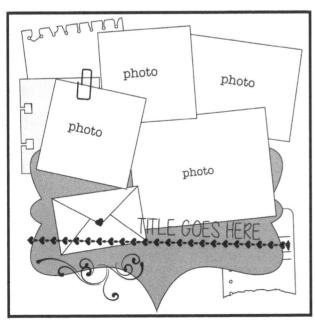
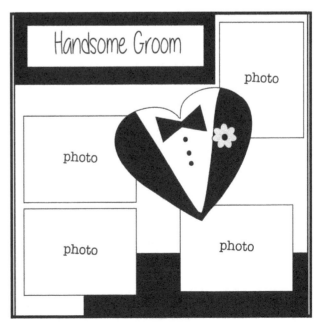

85

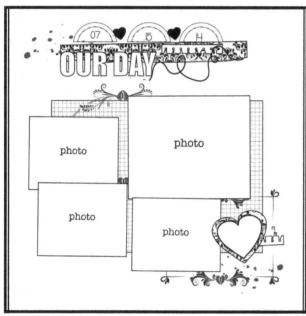
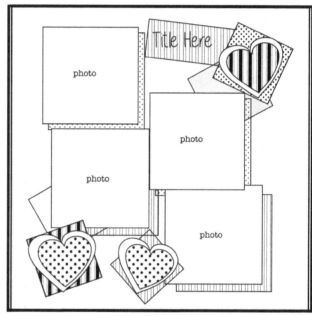
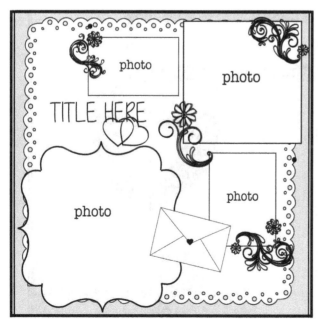
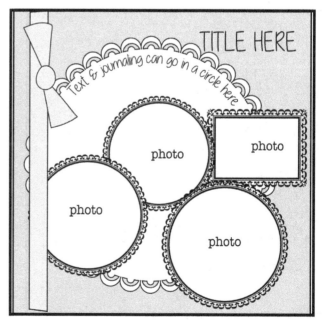

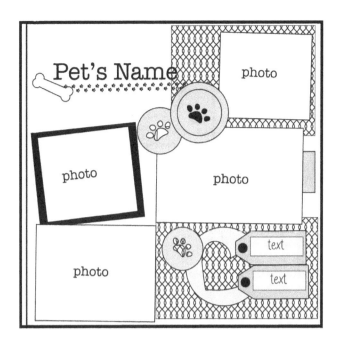
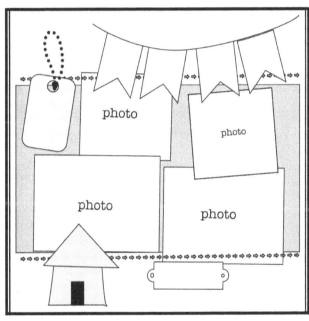
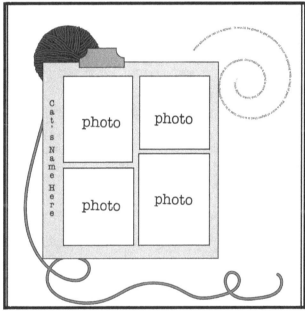
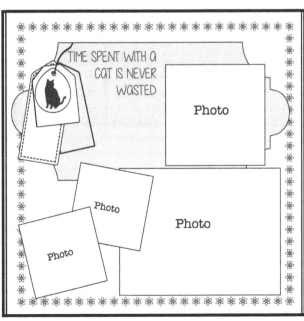
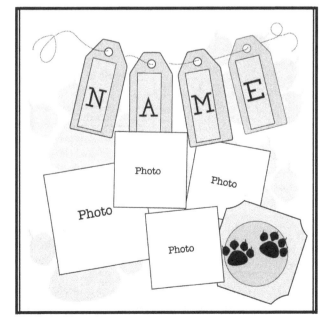

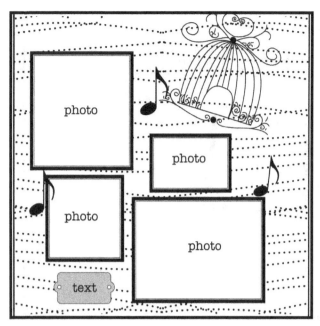
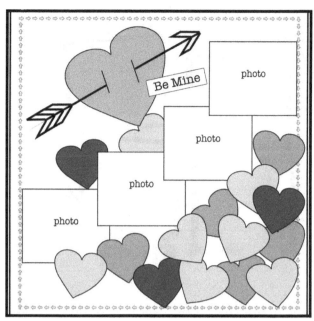
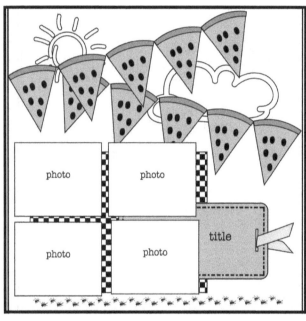

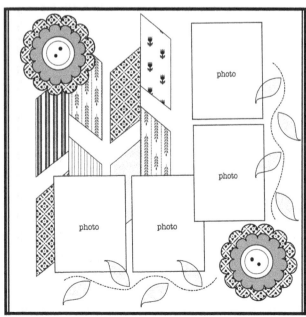
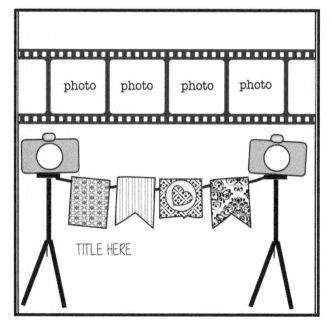

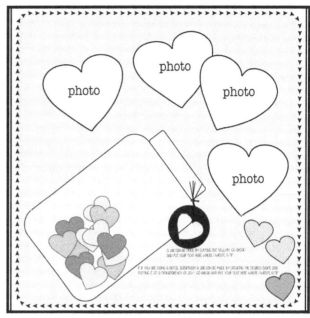
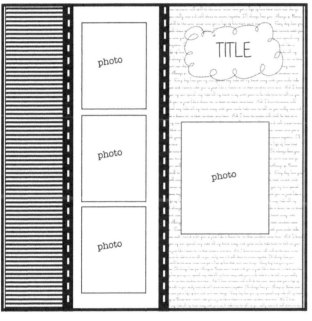
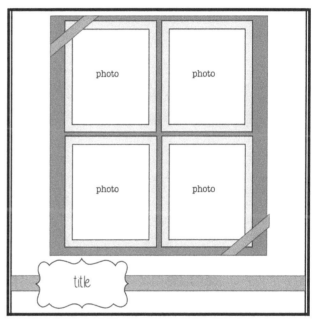
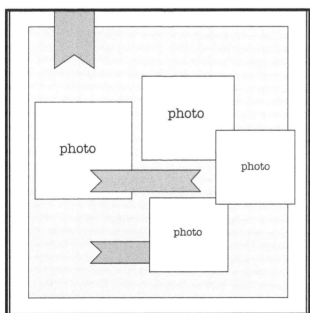
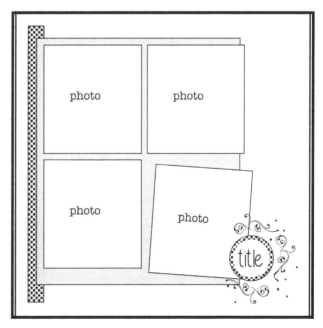

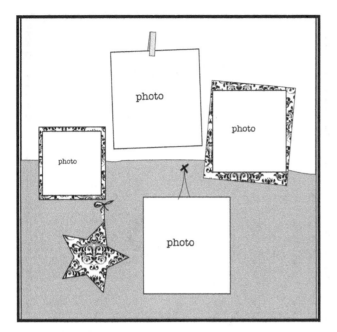
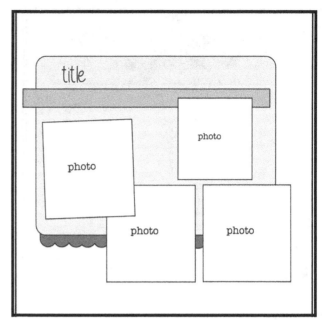
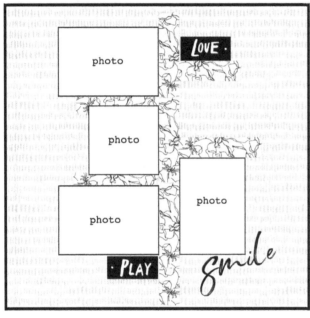

Double Page Sketches

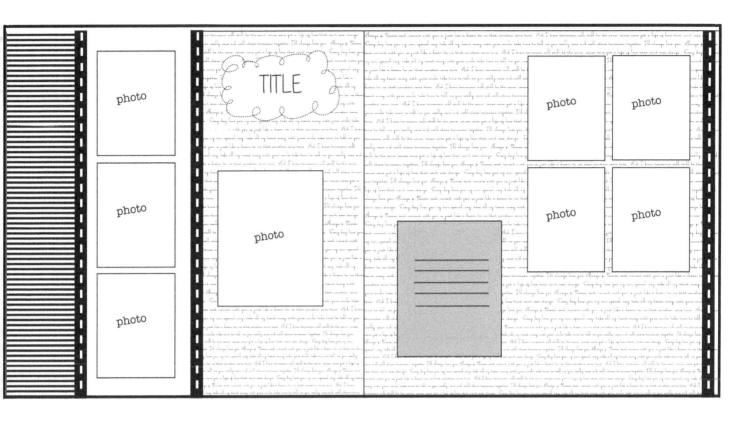

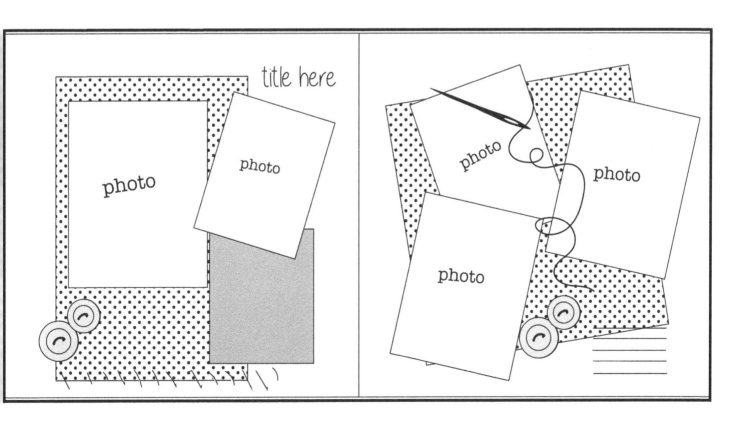

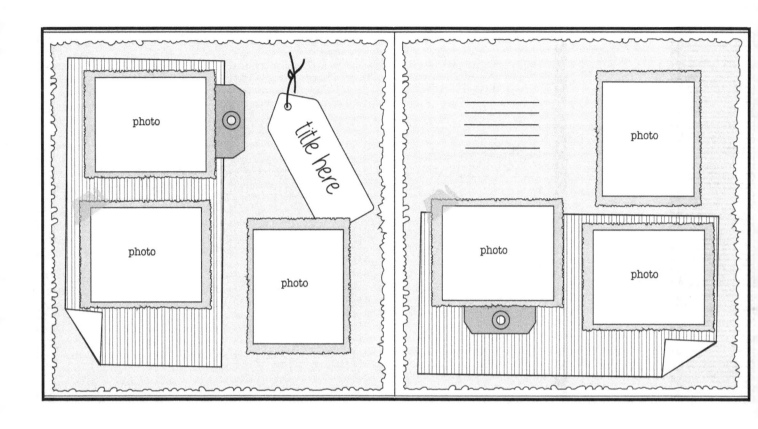

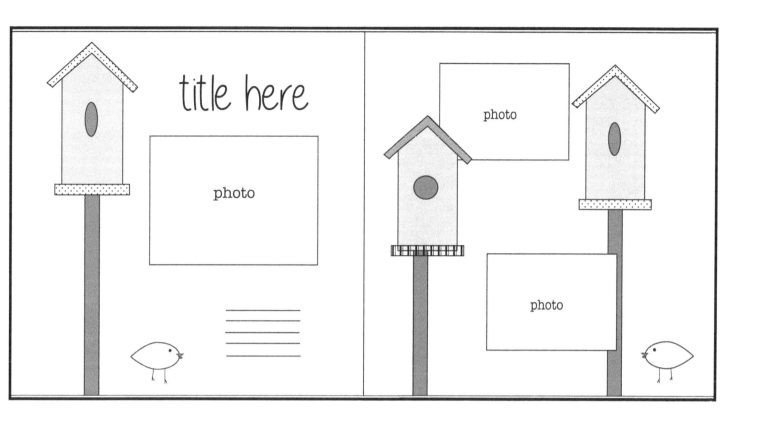
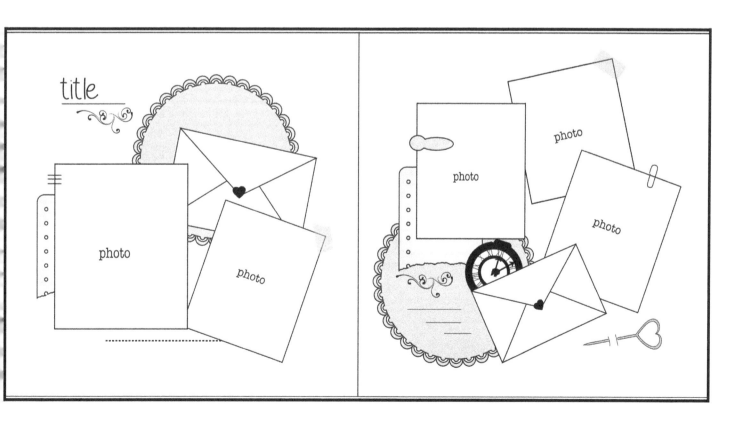

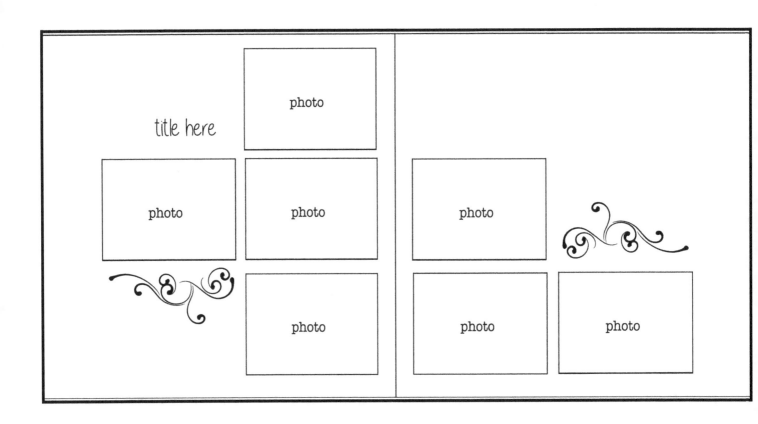
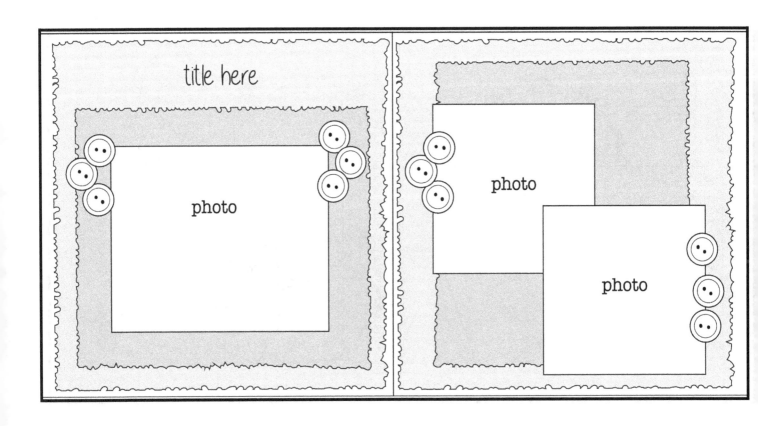

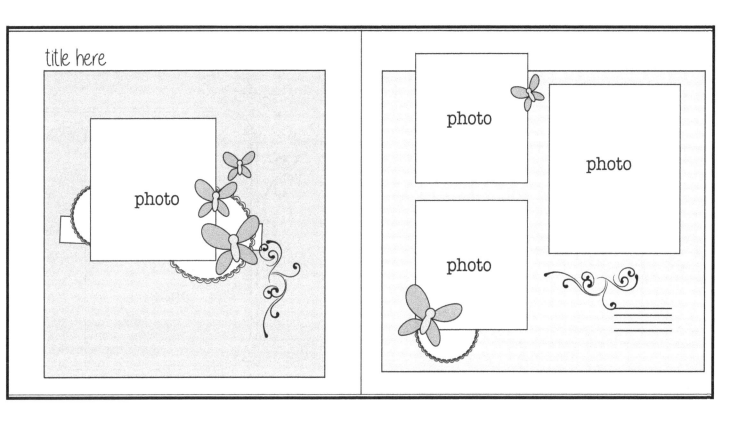
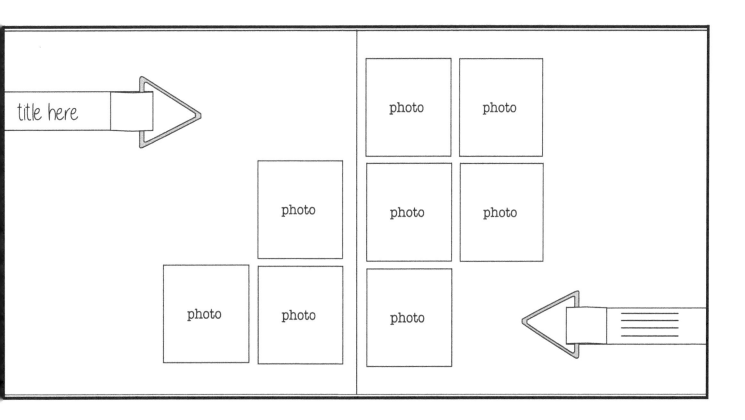

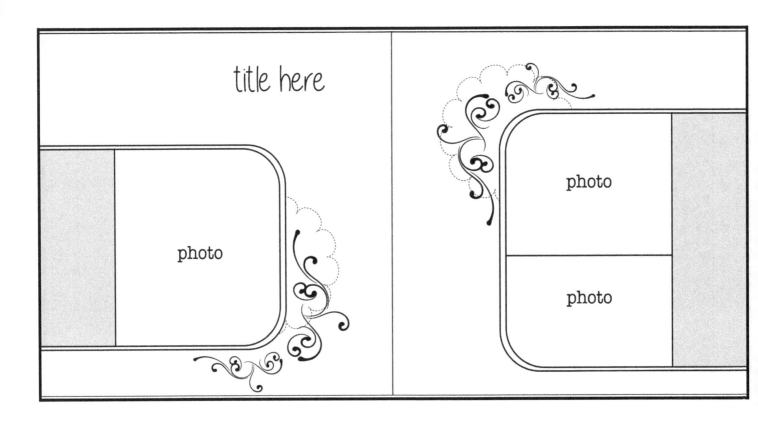
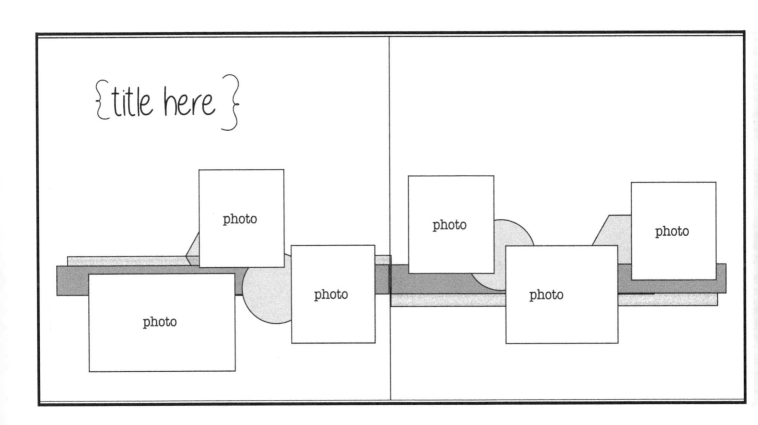

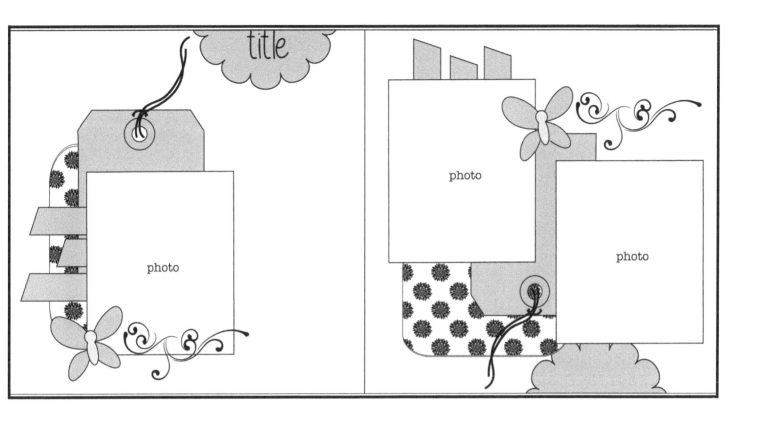
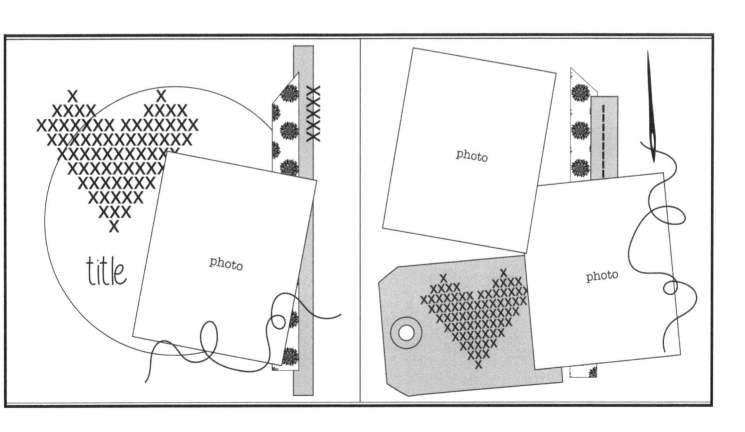

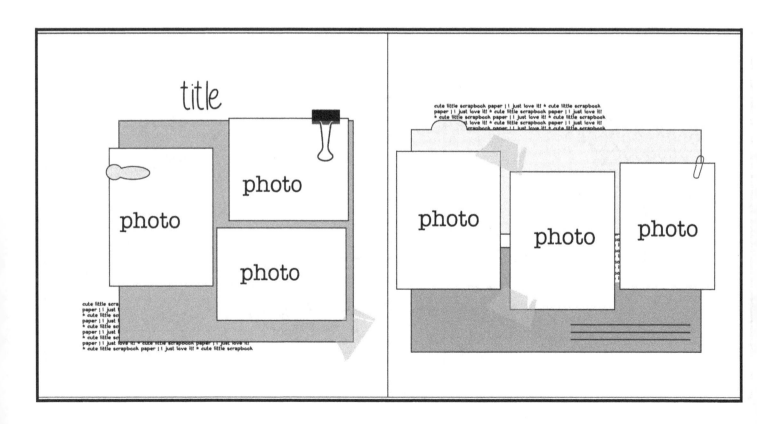

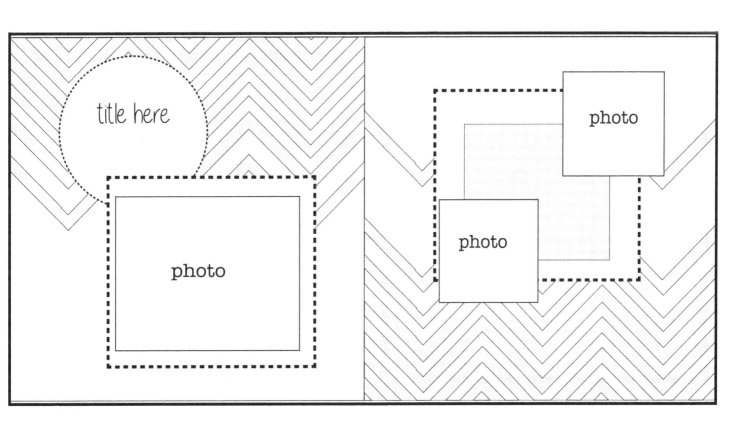

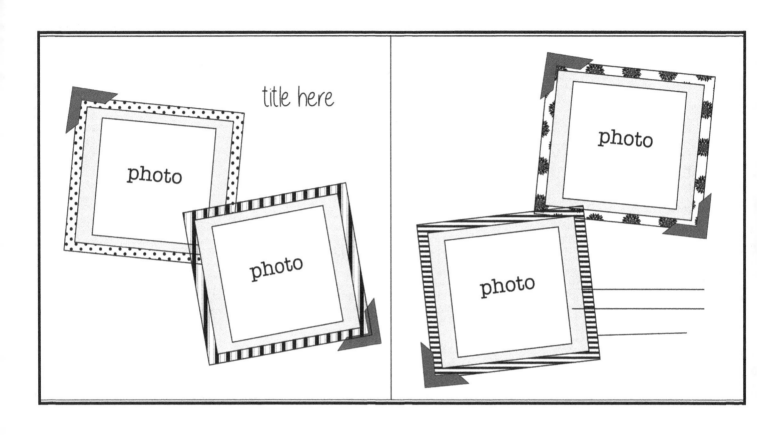
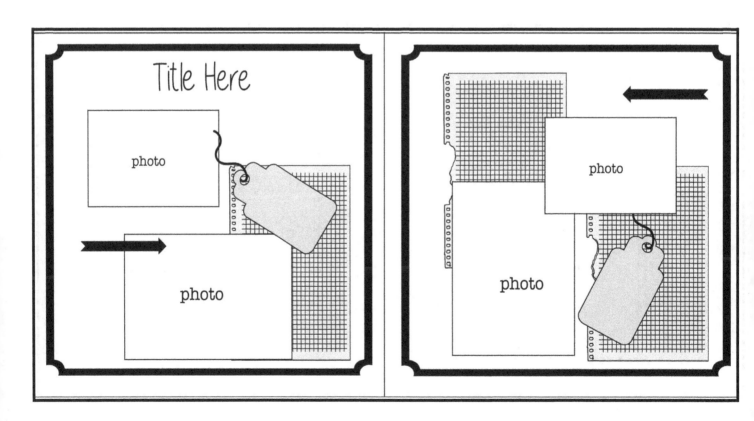